10 Things Members Should Know

MW01595163

10 Things Every Church Member Should Know

By

Anthony Collins

www.bookstandpublishing.com

Published by
Bookstand Publishing
Morgan Hill, CA 95037
4003_4

Tony Collins Ministries
P.O. Box 925
Lenoir City, TN 37771-0925
www.TonyCollinsMinistries.com

Copyright © 2013 by Anthony Collins
All rights reserved. No part of this publication may be reproduced or transmitted in any form or by any means, electronic or mechanical, including photocopy, recording, or any information storage and retrieval system, without permission in writing from the copyright owner.

ISBN 978-1-61863-623-2

Printed in the United States of America

Unless otherwise indicated, all Scripture references cited are taken from the Holy Bible, New International Version®, NIV® Copyright © 1973, 1978, 1984, 2011 by Biblica, Inc.® Used by permission. All rights reserved worldwide.

Scripture references marked NKJV® are taken from The Holy Bible, New King James Version Copyright © 1982 by Thomas Nelson, Inc.

Disclaimer: The exercises and charts in the appendices that follow were collected from numerous sources and speakers over the past twenty years of study and ministry, therefore attempts to provide accurate documentation proved difficult. If any readers recognize material contained in the appendices and can identify original sources, please contact the author, Anthony Collins, through his website, www.WeBeenlLiedTo.com, so source documentation may be added at the next printing.

Dedication

I dedicate this book to all of the members of the church universal who have been anointed by Jesus Christ to lead the church local. This is for those who see their service to the Lord as a ministry and not a committee, board, or job. To the ushers, nursery workers, greeters, hospitality workers, trustees, and stewards; to outreach, missions, and security teams; to Christian education workers, Bible study teachers, van drivers, parking lot attendants, janitors, and cooks; to special events teams, administrators, computer teams, and audio visual workers; to worship and praise teams, musicians, directors, and deacons; to finance teams, prayer intercessors, prayer groups, and small group leaders; to preachers, pastors, evangelists, apostles, all church leaders, and those who would like to become positive impact church leaders. I pray this book will provide some level of encouragement for us all to focus on the pertinent and significant to the glory of our Lord and King.

And to my daughter, Erica, whom I love dearly, I pray God's best for you in this life and the life to come. Never stop opening yourself up to the will of God for your life. Never stop questioning your motives. Never get comfortable with your relationship with Jesus Christ. Never stop requesting that He shine His holy light of inspection into the most uncomfortable areas of your life. Nothing will prevent me from loving you. Nothing will prevent me from praying God's best for you. Never stop believing that even in the midst of what appears a hopelessly desperate situation, Jesus calms the storm by simply speaking a few words.

Foreword

Church membership is an essential element when it comes to Christian mission, maturity, and ministry. It is a privilege and a blessing to be connected with a healthy local body of Christian believers. However, along with the blessing comes the responsibility for each member to grow and serve as followers of Jesus Christ. While the Bible gives us magnificent insights about the Christian church and her leadership, practical tools are often needed to carry out the assignment. Those who are planted in the house of the Lord will flourish when they become who God has designed them to be. *10 Things Every Church Member Should Know* makes a relevant contribution toward this spiritual objective.

Pastor Tony Collins is not only scriptural and spiritual in his approach in this text but is also practical. This book offers excellent ministry tools for those who are serious and intentional about growing disciples, developing leaders, and handling the business and ministry of the church with excellence. The practicality in this work is useful and suitable for any congregation. He guides us in becoming conscious of the fact that ministry is more about God and others than ourselves. A great truth revealed in this publication is this: church members must learn to love and respect each other, and at the same time learn to trust and obey God. As we serve one another, we must exemplify godly character. What a great reminder this is for the people of God!

Although the author offers ten things church members should know, the insight and spiritual nuggets you will find in this book are far greater. The power, purpose, and principles behind this effort will have a lasting effect on those who are readers and doers of the same. As I read through this book, I was reacquainted with the power of integrity, Christian example, stable leadership, committed church members, and good communication skills. Collins teaches us the importance of Christian maturity, relationship building, and team focus with ministry leaders and the congregation. As a result, he helps us to embrace the blessings of diversity through culture, gifts, talents, and personalities. We also learn from this author that we are not lone rangers in ministry but are ministry partners who serve together for the cause of Jesus Christ.

As Pastor Collins discusses conflict, we learn that although conflict is unavoidable, with wisdom, grace, and love it can be effectively handled. We are given practical exercises and gems to guide us in learning what every church member should know and doing what every church member and church leader should be doing for God's glory. We are guided through this masterpiece with wisdom for the common challenges that the church faces in such times as these. I believe that God has placed in the heart of Pastor Tony Collins a heart to see Christians and the church become transformed into the image of Jesus Christ and to begin to live victorious lives! It will not take long for you to discern his heart concerning spiritual matters and the Christian church.

I commend this work to you and recommend it as a resource for personal use, ministry equipping, team building, and congregational unity. As you read, it is my prayer, that you will be challenged, encouraged, and inspired, just as I was. It will bless any culture, communion, or congregation. What would become of us if we followed the instructions of this writer? What would really happen to the church if we all practiced what every church member should know? What a joy it would be if every member of our congregations or ministry team would read, study, and practice the teachings of this publication.

With the help of the Holy Spirit, we would renew our focus, redirect our passions, and restore our love for God and His people. This writing is divinely inspired, Christ-centered, and biblically rooted. What a blessed and wonderful gift *10 Things Every Church Member Should Know* is to the Body of Christ!"

Pastor Eric L. Leake
Flossmoor, Illinois

Table of Contents

Chapter 1: Choose the Right Leaders 1

Chapter 2: Become a Model of Positive Christian Leadership 7

Chapter 3: Think like an Authentic Christian 17

Chapter 4: Develop a Good Communication Process 31

Chapter 5: Foster an Atmosphere of Open Communication 39

Chapter 6: Focus on the Team 49

Chapter 7: Become a Great Team Member 63

Chapter 8: Value Diversity 73

Chapter 9: Seek to Effectively Handle Conflict 79

Chapter 10: Walk the Talk 93

Appendices

Appendix A   102

Appendix B   104

Appendix C   109

Appendix D   111

Appendix E   117

Opening Prayer

Lord Jesus, show me in what areas I have not been the church member You deserved. Help me to be completely open to the truth. I pray for openness and honesty to be prevalent as I read this book, and that I would receive whatever you have for me. Help me see what I can do to become a better church member and leader and to make my church better, for Your glory. Amen!

Chapter 1

Choose the Right Leaders

Does the quality of leadership make a significant difference in the results or outcomes of a group or organization? The obvious answer is yes. The purpose of this book is to help you become an individual with significant positive impact in any group or organization, especially the church. If this is not important to you, then put this book down and read something else. However, if you find this initial question important and you desire to have a positive impact on your church or organization, read on.

The position of leader, whether formal or informal, represents the privileged few selected to have influence over a group of people. *You do not need a title to be a leader.* Leaders will lead. Their leadership may be positive or negative, but all leaders lead their teams somewhere. The quality of a leader's ability to lead will go a long way in determining the quality of an organization. Most often, organizations reflect the character and priorities of their leaders, whether positive or negative. Whether you lead an usher ministry or a congregation, the same principles apply.

We have seen in many settings how a change in leadership resulted in dramatic change in the future of an organization. Chrysler, Google, and Coca-Cola immediately come to mind. Obviously, their new leaders had help turning these companies around. However, the vision for positive change and the skill set to put the vision in place must begin with the leader. An effective leader sets the tone for change. An effective leader fosters an environment of integrity, tolerance, patience, and love.

Those we choose as leaders help determine the success or failure of our organization based on the level and nature of their influence within the organization. As a result, it is critical that we choose high-quality leaders who will advance the goals and objectives of the organization in a way that has positive impact on individuals both inside and outside the organization.

How to Choose the Wrong Leaders

When choosing leaders, we should be aware of some natural tendencies to surround ourselves with those who make us comfortable. Additionally, we usually follow traditional standards of acceptance for leadership within any group or organization. Nothing is wrong, per se, with either of these approaches. However, be cautious that they are not the sole basis for making decisions about someone's capacity for positive leadership. Some of the following criteria used to choose leaders in the church have resulted in less than excellent results:

- The amount of their financial contribution to the church.
- The individual's position or standing within the community or how much influence they have within the community.
- Level of education.
- They are family or friends.
- They regularly attend church.

It is important to have people in leadership who are committed to the church, both through their time at church and giving to church. People of influence also can be a great help in providing access to resources every organization needs. In addition, nothing is inherently wrong with selecting family and/or friends for significant roles within ministry. However, if we are to have the best leaders in place, there must be an additional level of criteria.

Additional Criteria for Choosing Leaders

Do not rush to appoint a new leader or replace an old one. Take your time and remain systematic throughout the process. Stay diligent, but most important stay biblical in the process. Here are some significant criteria to consider as you determine who is qualified to lead:

- A believer. Within the church, you must be a believer to qualify to lead ministries. You must have a personal relationship with Jesus Christ.
- Understand and support the church vision.
- Commitment to the Word of God. Potential church leaders must allow the Word of Jesus Christ to shape and mold their lives.
- Commitment to the house of God. A qualified church leader exhibits this commitment through giving time and finances to the church.
- Commitment to those in church leadership. Leaders should be respectful of spiritual authority and willing to give honor where honor is due.
- Commitment to the activities necessary to do the job well.
- Void of selfish volunteerism. They do not think they are doing the church a favor by working in a ministry.
- Void of consumerism. They are not at church because of what they can consume from the church.
- Strong during adversity. Qualified church leaders are not crybabies or easily discouraged when they do not get their way or because they do not agree with every decision. They do not leave because things get a little uncomfortable. They also will not

3

leave to avoid the conviction of the Holy Spirit or to avoid reconciliation.

- Quick to forgive and quick to ask for forgiveness.
- Quick to say, "I'm sorry."
- Teachable. Those with a spirit that is not open to accountability are not qualified to lead. This characteristic is so important that a leadership candidate may not have some of the other traits of excellent leaders, but if teachable, they can learn them.
- Humble. Anyone who has an arrogant, prideful, manipulative spirit of control is not qualified to lead in any way.
- A good communicator. Good leaders don't have to be professional speakers, but they do need to be able to talk with people and communicate ideas in a way that doesn't hinder the progress of the organization.
- Not afraid of confrontation. Depending on the leadership position, lack of this trait can also be an automatic disqualifier. Life is full of resistance. Certainly there is opposition and defiance in the church. Whenever we would do that which is good, evil is always present. Individuals who are unwilling to stand up for what is right, as outlined in the Holy Bible, in a spirit of love and humility, are not suited for many ministry leadership positions.
- Concerned about achieving organizational goals, but more concerned about the people than the organization. It is good to have focus on organizational objectives, but best to focus on people, to focus on what best accomplishes Christ's purpose of advancing the Kingdom of heaven now, here on earth. Christ came for the people, not for an

organization. The organization is not as important as the people. Without people, the organization ceases to exist.

- Open to continuous improvement.
- Diverse. Diversity matters to Jesus Christ, which is obvious in the many different types of people He created. Look for leadership candidates who don't think like you think, who don't have your same background or upbringing, and people who don't look or act like you. Your leadership team will be stronger as a result.
- Creativity and innovation—the ability to think outside the normal thought process. Good leadership candidates are not bound by the barriers of tradition; they are open thinkers, within the confines of the Bible.
- Attention to detail through planning and organization.
- Adaptability—the ability to be flexible in different situations while dealing with different personalities, but still getting the job done.
- Ability to build personal relationships with people on several levels.
- Good judgment and decision making.
- Emotional intelligence or self-awareness—an understanding of how their actions affect those around them.

Choose leaders based on biblical principles and expect them to live their lives based on those principles. Seeking out these criteria above will lead you to the most qualified leadership candidates for ministries in your church.

Those who guide this people mislead them,
and those who are guided are led astray.
                              Isaiah 9:16

"And whoever wants to be first must be your
slave—just as the Son of Man did not come
to be served, but to serve, and to give his life
as a ransom for many."
                              Matthew 20:27–28

"Leave them; they are blind guides."
                              Matthew 15:14

Live the life you want to live. Be the person you want to remember.

6

Chapter 2

Become a Model of Positive Christian Leadership

What do quality Christian leaders look like when you see them function in their assigned roles? They lead and minister with the heart of a servant. They catch people doing things well and they encourage them. They respond to people not performing up to their capacity by exhorting them to be their best. Quality leaders are able to make allowances for others while maintaining their stance on the Word of God. They are leaders in love—in love for the Lord Jesus Christ and in love for others.

> *Love is patient, love is kind. It does not envy, it does not boast, it is not proud. It does not dishonor others, it is not self-seeking, it is not easily angered, it keeps no record of wrongs. Love does not delight in evil but rejoices with the truth. It always protects, always trusts, always hopes, always perseveres.*
> 1 Corinthians 13:4–6

Leadership Is Important

Quality Christian leadership is crucial not simply because it provides the best opportunity for an organization to excel but also because it allows the church the greatest prospect to accomplish its mission as outlined by Jesus Christ in Matthew 28:19, "Therefore go and make disciples of all nations, baptizing them in the name of the Father and of the Son and of the Holy Spirit."

Through those who lead in love, and show others how to lead in love, the Holy Spirit proves the authenticity of our Lord Jesus Christ. How do we provide proof to the world that Jesus is real and that we are His representatives here on earth? Not by the size of our churches or the number of ministry programs we have implemented. The proof is simply whether we love each other the way Christ has loved us—without regard for ethnicity, economic status, social standing, or anything else. Love unconditionally. Love unpredictably. Love unreservedly.

> *"A new command I give you: Love one another. As I have loved you, so you must love one another. By this everyone will know that you are my disciples, if you love one another."*
>
> John 13:34–35

Through such love the church body, both local and universal, is fortified. Through Christ's love we can best provide for the church body that which is most excellent, as required by the Holy Scriptures.

Excellent Leadership—a Poor Example

Let's examine what ineffective leadership looks like. To do this, we will consider Israel's leadership responses to the nation's first opportunity to enter the Promised Land. In the book of Numbers in the Holy Bible, the nation of Israel, after having been delivered from Egypt, has finally made it to the border of Canaan—the land of promise, the land that Jehovah God promised Abraham in His covenant with him as the father of the nation of Israel. The thirteenth chapter of Numbers represents a critical time in the life of this nation. It is the response of leadership that will determine the ultimate destiny of many and the immediate destiny of everyone that is part of this great nation.

At the end of forty days they returned from exploring the land. They came back to Moses and Aaron and the whole Israelite community at Kadesh in the Desert of Paran. There they reported to them and to the whole assembly and showed them the fruit of the land. They gave Moses this account: "We went into the land to which you sent us, and it does flow with milk and honey! Here is its fruit. But the people who live there are powerful, and the cities are fortified and very large. We even saw descendants of Anak there. The Amalekites live in the Negev; the Hittites, Jebusites and Amorites live in the hill country; and the Canaanites live near the sea and along the Jordan." Then Caleb silenced the people before Moses and said, "We should go up and take possession of the land, for we can certainly do it." But the men who had gone up with him said, "We can't attack those people; they are stronger than we are." And they spread among the Israelites a bad report about the land they had explored. They said, "The land we explored devours those living in it. All the people we saw there are of great size. We saw the Nephilim there (the descendants of Anak come from the Nephilim). We seemed like grasshoppers in our own eyes, and we looked the same to them."

Numbers 13:25–33

Based on the example of the majority of these Israelite "leaders" who brought back a report on the Promised Land to God's people, let us examine the functionality of poor quality leaders:

- They have more focus on what they see, hear, and feel in the natural than on the Word of God. This is a perpetual weakness among poor leaders. No matter how much of God's Word they know, they are too easily dissuaded from standing on it, depending instead upon the circumstances. They allow surrounding conditions to tell them about their God, not the reverse. If a task is difficult, if it requires them moving too far out of their comfort zones, then regardless of what God's Word says, they are not moving forward.
- They have low spiritual self-esteem. Don't confuse humility with a broken sense of self. Divine-ordered humility will never prevent or get in the way of us obeying God's commands and fulfilling His will for our lives. Humility is needed, but what is just as important is knowing who we are in Christ, our spiritual position in Him. We *are not* who we think we are, unless who we think we are is who Christ says we are. We *are* who Christ says we are. It is time that leaders begin to believe the Word of God to the point of action regarding who we are in Him. Here are a few of these truths:

  1. We are God's children (John 1:12).
  2. We are Christ's friends (John 15:15).
  3. We are united with the Lord (1 Corinthians 6:17).
  4. We are saints (Ephesians 1:1).

5. We are complete in Christ Jesus (Colossians 2:10).
6. We have assurance that everything works together for our good (Romans 8:28).
7. We cannot be separated from the love of Christ Jesus (Romans 8:35–39).
8. We are established, anointed, and sealed by God (2 Corinthians 1:21-22).
9. We have not been given a spirit of fear, but of power, love, and a sound mind (2 Timothy 1:7).
10. We are born of God, and the evil one cannot touch us (1 John 5:18).
11. We have been chosen and appointed to bear good spiritual fruit (John 15:16).
12. We can do all the things Christ has commanded us to do (Philippians 4:13).

We must meditate upon these biblical truths as leaders to the point that they change our thought processes and ultimately our actions.

- Poor quality leaders are problem focused instead of solution focused. They overemphasize their weaknesses and their enemy's strengths. Instead of relying on the power of God, they have no confidence in God's ability, and no confidence in themselves and who they are in Christ. They see their personal weakness as the reason why they can't and won't be successful. They magnify the problem and completely discount the power of God.
- They are more afraid of men than of God. The number-one command in the Bible is "Don't be afraid" or "Fear not." Why? Because God knows that what we fear we will ultimately worship. When

we fear anything more than we do God's Word and His will for our lives, we have moved God from His place as first. We have become idolaters. In that moment we have lost our ability to function as positive Christian leaders, no matter what the situation.

- They have no real confidence in the faithfulness of God's Word. Even though these Israelite leaders had personally witnessed the power of God, they were unwilling to trust God in their current situations. They were more focused on the "what ifs" of the circumstances than on what they already knew through their experience with God. They thought, "What if God doesn't do what He says He's going to do? All that I love will be lost." We must choose to willingly do what God says, even when victory doesn't look like we think it should. It is a choice to trust Christ's Word, His promises, in spite of what our eyes see, our ears hear, and our heart feels. It is a choice to allow the power of His Word and His Spirit to override our natural tendencies and move forward in faith. Only in making this right choice in this moment can we authentically show our love for Christ through obedience.

- They have a spirit of "can't," even in light of God saying they can. Our spiritual enemy is always probing us, especially in difficult situations, to determine "What is the price for us to say no to Jesus?" Far too many of us serve the gods of comfort, convenience, and predictability. The moment Jesus requires us to do something uncomfortable, inconvenient, or unpredictable, we are quick to say no. As followers of Jesus Christ, and most assuredly as leaders within the body of

Christ, we do not have the right to say no when Christ has already said yes.

- They stir people instead of calming people. The job of a good leader is to develop within the group or organization a focus on God's Word—first. The response of the leader, and ultimately the response of the group, must be one that honors God's Word and brings glory to Jesus Christ. A calm and composed focus on God's Word will calm a Christian church, organization, or group. When Christian leaders, with a sense of purpose and resolve, focus their response to any situation based on the power and authority of God's Word, it will provide peace in the midst of a chaotic situation. When leaders focus on God's Word, then harmony, unity, and peace is constructed within the body of Christ.

Excellent Leadership—Good Example

In the above Scripture passage, Caleb exhibits the qualities we should look for in our church leadership. He says only what God has already said; he agrees with God. Caleb exhibits the following positive leadership traits that we should seek for our churches and ministry teams:

- His focus is on the Word of God first, and everything else is second. Caleb understands that there are challenges. He has not put his head in the sand and pretended that this will not be a fight, yet he knows what God has said and has chosen to walk in faith, declaring the victory God already promised.
- He knows what he is capable of with God and therefore knows he has nothing to fear. He knows

that it is his enemy that needs to be afraid. He knows that because God is with him, victory is assured.

- He is not afraid of his enemy in the land of Canaan or afraid of his peers. He knows what God's Word says and is committed to that and that alone.
- He has a clear memory of all God has already done in his life, which gives him confidence that God will continue to be faithful to His Word.
- The task before him is daunting. Israel is grossly outnumbered and in unfamiliar geography. They are only recently emancipated slaves, and most certainly are not warriors. But in spite of what seems impossible in the natural, Caleb understands that if God says he can, he can. Because God does not have the word *impossible* in His vocabulary, Caleb has chosen to eliminate it from his.
- Because of all of the above, Caleb is unable to keep silent. He becomes a quieting force for truth and a beacon for the will of God in the midst of a group of fearful people, absorbed with themselves and what they want.

Good vs. Great

Top quality leaders have a big-picture vision of their future and the future of their group, church, or organization. They have the ability to make decisions and speak with a focus beyond what is immediately needed or seen. They can speak and direct their team members to concentrate on those things that build the group toward excellence long-term. Below you will find a few examples of how good leaders can become great leaders:

- Good leaders get results primarily directing people and getting their cooperation. Great leaders involve people in the process and help them invest their personal commitment.
- Good leaders build good followers. Great leaders build good leaders.
- Good leaders manage people one-on-one. Great leaders build collaborative, interdependent, and supportive teams.
- Good leaders develop strength within their own ministry unit. Great leaders develop strength between ministry units and peers.
- Good leaders implement direction from their supervisors. Great leaders initiate new ideas and direction.
- Good leaders help people change when directed and help them make the most of it. Great leaders generate positive innovations without those changes being imposed from their managers.
- Good leaders communicate well. Great leaders become masterful at interpersonal relationships.

Do you know whether or not you are a good leader? How can you make an accurate determination? Much of your assessment should focus on the level of trust your team and those in your peer group have in you. Take a look at the assessment in appendix A, "How Much Should Your Team Trust You?" Fill out the answers yourself, as best you can, from your team's and peers' perspectives. Then if you really want to know the truth, have your team and peers fill out the assessment on you, anonymously. Use the feedback to help you develop a proactive strategy for improvement.

Live the life you want to live. Be the person you want to remember.

Chapter 3

Think Like an Authentic Christian

*Do not conform to the pattern of this world,
but be transformed by the renewing of your
mind. Then you will be able to test and
approve what God's will is—his good,
pleasing and perfect will.*

Romans 12:2

The focal point in the battle to become an excellent leader
is in our minds. As a man thinks, so he is. Whatever we
believe determines our actions. What we believe is
determined by what we do with the thoughts that come into
our minds.

There are many instances in the Bible where the
devil brought an evil thought into the mind of righteous
people. David was incited by evil to take a census, and
seventy thousand people died (1 Chronicles 21:1). Judas
was influenced by an evil thought and betrayed Jesus and
then committed suicide (John 13:27). Evil filled the minds
of Ananias and Sapphira and it cost them their lives (Acts
5:3). The enemy attacked Eve's mind (Genesis 3:1), and
with Adam as her accomplice, they sold their birthright of
authority and dominion over the earth to Satan.

From the beginning of time as we know it, down
through the ages and even now, evil attacks our minds with
subtle thoughts. We believe these thoughts are our
thoughts, because if we didn't, we would never be
deceived. We act on these thoughts without filtering them
through the Word of God, because they seem unnecessary
to be taken captive to God's Word. We think our thoughts
are too innocent for the biblical filter. I can hear David say,
"What's wrong with taking a census?" I can hear Eve say,

"What's wrong with having more knowledge?" I can hear Judas say, "What could be wrong in hurrying along Jesus' reign on earth?"

What's wrong is that these ideas have not been filtered through the Word of God. What's wrong is that these ideas, no matter how subtle or seemingly innocent, did not originate from God, so they cannot honor God. This means that by necessity, their fulfillment must end in disaster.

When we believe a lie, that belief does not impact simply one decision. Typically, that first decision leads to another decision and then another. Because the foundation of all these decisions is a lie, the further you get away from the first decision based on a lie, the more disastrous the potential outcome. The only way to correct the real problem is to return to the original false belief and correct it. This will have a self-correcting effect on all the subsequent decisions.

Good leaders have the truth at their very core—the absolute truth of God's Word. They know and believe the Word of God; this is evident by their behavior. Many people know God's Word intellectually but do not believe it to the point of action. You can see this in their lifestyles. It is imperative that leaders be good models of what it means to be obedient to God's commands. They have taken the Word of God literally and are not easily deceived. These leaders are able to determine if a thought is from God or from the realm of evil.

And we take captive every thought to make it obedient to Christ.
2 Corinthians 10:5

A Positive "Will Do" Attitude

When our core is the truth, it is much easier to have a positive attitude. The truth inside of us will reveal itself, especially in difficult times. That revelation will be in the form of a positive attitude. We will think like authentic Christians.

We cannot control most of the things that happen in our lives. The idea of control is an illusion, a trick, a lie from the pit of hell. We are not in control; God is in control. But there is at least one thing we can control—our attitude. We can control how we respond to life's situations and make positive, God-honoring choices.

Good leaders choose to respond to life's predicaments with a positive attitude. This attitude simply applies the Word of God to every situation. Whatever God says is what a good leader says. And because God is always positive, because God is always speaking life, because God is an encourager, this leader will say and become these things as well. God will use the truth inside of such a leader, and the confidence in Christ it produces, to inspire others to be encouraged. He will use this leader to increase the capacity of those they are around to also walk in faith according to the Word of God.

Some of the attitudinal characteristics of this good leader are:

- *Appreciation.* These individuals have an attitude of gratefulness. They understand that no matter the situation, they are blessed. They are quick to see the glass as half full.
- *Victory.* Even in difficult situations and circumstances, they have a spirit of celebration and success. They understand that God uses the trials of

life to fortify us spiritually and to bring Himself glory.

- *Calm.* Many things will get these individuals excited (praise, worship, good teaching, souls saved, etc.), but what will not phase them is adversity. In the midst of life's storms, these individuals bring to themselves and others a recollection of the promises of God. God's promises bring a peace that surpasses all understanding.
- *Belief in a positive outcome.* When faced with two possible conclusions to a problem, these individuals believe that the most positive outcome will be the result. And they are usually right.
- *Pleasant to be around.* As a result of all of the above, while not perfect, good leaders are a pleasure to be around. They usually have a smile and a positive word for all they come in contact with.

When we think like an authentic Christian, it is impossible for us not to act like one as well.

You Are Killing Me

The opposite of these positive wonderful leaders who encourage and build us up are those individuals who have a debilitating effect on those they come in contact with. This is especially true during difficult circumstances. These negative "no way we can do that" individuals have a difficult time applying God's Word to their lives. They may know God's Word, and even believe it on a cerebral level, but they have extreme difficulty applying His Word to their personal lives. There is a disconnection between their understanding and their behavior. These individuals usually exhibit the following attitudes and attributes:

- *Critical spirit.* There is always something wrong, something to complain about. If only things weren't this way or that, then everything would be alright. These individuals love to stir the people. They cannot be counted upon in times of adversity.
- *Victim mentality.* These individuals insist that they have been deeply hurt, offended, and mistreated. They are quick to point out their woundedness at the expense of addressing their waywardness. They have no hesitation in declaring that they deserve "better than this."
- *Drama king or queen.* These people are experts in creating a crisis out of the smallest incident. To them the whole world is a stage, and they are not going to be upstaged by anyone. They take every available chance to be emotional and do their best to get an emotional response out of those around them.
- *Believe the worst possible outcome will prevail.* No matter what the odds, or how positive the trends might be, these individuals dwell on the negative, sometimes to the point of paralysis.
- *Bitterness.* These people hold grudges and have a resentful spirit. They do not carry the spirit of forgiveness. You may not see this bitterness until you cross them or get on their sensitive side. But it is there, and it will show itself at the most inopportune time.

Attitude Adjustment Needed

In the trials of life, we will process the information around us based on our past experiences and our current attitude. Our attitudes are determined by what filter we use on the thoughts that enter our minds. What we believe determines our attitudes. Our attitudes determine how we respond to the information in our current trial. Our response determines our behavior. Our behavior determines our legacy and our destiny. If you want to change your destiny, you must change your attitude, or change what you believe. Change what you allow yourself to hold onto. Change what you focus and meditate on. If you want to change your behavior, and change your legacy, you must change what you believe, change your attitude. If you want to change someone's behavior, don't focus on that person's behavior. Focus on addressing what they believe.

> *You can live opposite of what you profess, but you cannot live opposite of what you believe.*
>
> Dallas Willard
> Professor and Christian author

An Example

Company XYZ was having some financial difficulties, and it was rumored that layoffs were coming soon. Two midlevel managers, John and Pedro, were told on Monday that they had to meet with their managers late the following Friday. Both had a great deal of anxiety as they left work Monday afternoon.

John's response was negative self-talk. He immediately thought of the worst-case scenario and concluded that he was probably going to be laid off on Friday. He saw himself as a victim and became critical of everyone and everything that was work related. He wondered how they could let him go after all the hard work he had done. He had stayed late when he did not have to. He had volunteered to train new employees, which was not part of his job description. He went on and on, in his mind. He was sure he did not deserve to be dismissed. As the week went along, he became more and more angry and bitter. Finally John could not take it anymore. He was not going to give them the opportunity to fire him. He went into his supervisor's office on Wednesday afternoon and resigned.

Pedro, on the other hand, was a manager with a different spirit. Pedro was full of positive self-talk. While he realized the possibility of being laid off, he was not overanxious regarding that prospect. He thought about the great times he had experienced. He thought about how much he had learned. He thought about how blessed he was to have a position like this one. He knew if he was laid off, he was well equipped to get another job. He was confident that God would take care of him. He had a spirit of thankfulness about all Christ had done in his life. When the topic came up with his peers or coworkers, he was quick to share his viewpoint, his positive attitude, and his reassurance that regardless of the outcome, everything was going to be alright. Many of his fellow workers discussed how much they needed and appreciated Pedro's perspective during this trying period.

On Friday afternoon Pedro went into his supervisor's office. His manager told him how valuable he was. He wanted him to know that the layoffs would only affect some areas of the company not directly related to their division. Not only that, but Pedro was getting a promotion because of his hard work and positive attitude. His manager also wanted to know if Pedro had any insight as to why John had resigned. The company had been looking forward to promoting him with their next line expansion in a few months.

The question screaming to be asked is, "Are you John or are you Pedro?" Do you think like an authentic Christian?

Fortify Your Authentic Christian Attitude

If you desire to build and maintain a positive authentic Christian attitude, here are a few ideas:

1. *Positive self-talk.* Words are power. Whatever we tell ourselves (self-talk) impacts how we behave. God's Word tells us, "The tongue has the power of life and death" (Proverbs 18:21). This truth is seen in the biblical principle of "manifestation." God tells us if we want something to happen according to His Word, we should "believe in your heart and confess [or say it] with your mouth" (Romans 10:9–10). When we believe what God says, big things will happen. When we speak God's Word and believe it, things happen both in the spiritual and in the natural. The supernatural is birthed in our lives. Some biblically based, positive self-talk includes, but is not limited to phrases like:

   - No matter what I am going through, this will be for my benefit in the end.
   - I am blessed. Even in this situation I have a reason to be thankful.
   - I win regardless of the outcome of this situation, in Christ Jesus.
   - I can make a positive difference.

   These are but a few of the positive self-talk phrases you can use, based on God's Word. How many additional positive self talk phrases can you think of right now?

2. *Own the truth about yourself.* Don't overlook the areas in your life where you walk outside of God's Word and will for your life. Be quick to examine yourself according to the Word of God. Be quick to agree with God and make the necessary changes in your beliefs to facilitate a change in your behavior.
3. *Live in the now.* Be present in the moment you have now. Make the most of each opportunity. Don't allow negative thoughts and negative people to rob you of the precious joy and pleasure of the moment of now.
4. *Understand that an authentic Christian attitude is a choice.* We decide what we will do with the thoughts that come into our minds. We choose what we will believe. We choose to have the attitude of a Christian champion, or we choose to allow negative self-talk to fill our minds and destroy our destiny.
5. *Reprogram your mental computer every day with the Word of God.* No matter who we are, we need to continually read and listen to the Word of the Lord. This will allow us to hide His Word in our hearts, so that at the appropriate time, when it is needed the most, it will come out and help us be the leaders God has established us to be in His Spirit.

Positive Christian Attitude Killers

You can do some things that will absolutely destroy your authentic Christian attitude. First is negative self-talk. Some examples of meditating on negative self-talk are:

- *Living in the negative past.* This version of negative self-talk is always accompanied by the phrase "If only." If only something had happened differently, then you wouldn't be in your current bad situation. If you are meditating on these types of thoughts— dismiss them. You won't need them anymore, so send them away, in Jesus' name. You may have to perform the exercise of dismissing them several times. That's alright, just keep dismissing them, and eventually they will get the message.
- *Living in the negative present.* You are consumed with the problem at hand and worried about the outcome. You are sure the results are going to be negative, so the potential consequences of those negative results are eating you up inside. You wonder, "What am I going to do now?" Stop! Take a deep breath and prepare to deal positively with the problem. What is your responsibility in the situation? Have you fulfilled your responsibility? If not, then do so immediately. If you have, there is nothing more in the natural you can do. You are not responsible for, nor can you control, the actions of others. Next, what does God's Word say about the situation? If you know what God says about the situation, then say what His Word says and nothing else. Believe to the point of action that God will be faithful to His Word, and then prepare to be blessed.
- *Living in the negative future.* We can paint a thousand "what if" scenarios. Typically 99 percent of the things we worry about never come to pass. If you are stuck in the "what ifs" of life, then devise a positive plan to handle them.

The second way to destroy a positive Christian attitude is the unwillingness to own the truth about who you are and how your thoughts and actions affect you and those around you. We all have a natural tendency to think more highly of ourselves than we should. Because of this, we find it difficult to accept the truth when we are wrong or out of order. We should look to view our attitudes, actions, and motives through the eyes of Christ. This will allow us to stop pretending to be someone we are not and own the truth about who we really are. This will position us to have a more positive effect on those with whom we come in contact, and give us a more authentic testimony about Jesus.

Third is the unwillingness to believe that an authentic Christian attitude is a choice. You can control the negative self-talk and you can control the willingness to own the truth about yourself. The question is, "Will you?" It's your choice. It's not controlled by anyone except you.

Your Time Is Now

God is always preparing us. He is always looking for ways to bless us and take us to a higher level of knowledge, understanding, and wisdom in Him. God is much more concerned with our *hereafter* than He is with our *here and now*. He is always preparing us to be more and more like Him.

God is always testing us. Through our testing we prove to ourselves and all of creation that we are indeed ready for the blessing we have cried out to God for these many days. Every great leader will be tested, over and over again. Abraham was tested. David was tested. Joseph, Esther, even Christ was tested, that He might prove His obedience. Faith that is not tested is not worth much. The great things of God, the precious possessions of the Kingdom, can only be entrusted to those who have passed a vigorous period of testing.

God is always blessing. In the midst of the preparation and the testing, our God is blessing. He is blessing even when it appears His movements cannot be seen. It is His nature to bless, and He is constantly pouring out His love, mercy, grace, and goodness on the lives of the just and the unjust.

It is time for you to become an authentic Christian—not just someone who is a fan of Jesus Christ but someone who is committed to live a life according to His Word and will, regardless of the consequences. It is time for you to live the life you want to live, the life you know you should live. Decide today to be the person that you want people to remember.

What They Said

People are always blaming their circumstances for what they are.

George Bernard Shaw
Irish playwright

A positive attitude causes a chain reaction of positive thoughts, events and outcomes. It is a catalyst and it sparks extraordinary results.

Wade Boggs
Former professional baseball player

The power of one, if fearless and focused, is formidable.

Gloria Macapagai Arroyo
14th president of the Philippines

Are you wondering if you have the attitude of an authentic Christian? Take the Christian attitude assessment found in appendix B, "Do You Have a Positive Christian Attitude?" After you have taken it and recorded your score, come back to the end of this chapter. Take some time to evaluate your current attitude and make a commitment to do a few things differently to have a more positive impact in your family, on your job, and in your ministry.

What three things are you willing to do today to show the attitude of an authentic Christian?

_____

_____

_____

Live the life you want to live. Be the person you want to remember.

Chapter 4

Develop a Good Communication Process

I know that you believe you understand what you think I said, but I'm not sure realize that what you heard is not what I meant.
Robert McCloskey
Children's book author and illustrator

The communication process is simple in explanation, but complicated in practice. The *sender* (the person talking) encodes a *message* (using words) and sends it to the *receiver* (the person listening). The receiver then gives some level of feedback to the sender to acknowledge that the message was received.

While this process is relatively simple, it is also extremely difficult to accomplish with excellence. The reason for this is that we speak in words, but we hear in images. We take the words we hear and turn them into images. These images are affected by our temperament, character, personality, experiences, and current conditions. It is important to take these points into consideration when you determine how you will reach your intended audience. One word can have more than one meaning, depending on the audience. Your effectiveness as an organization will depend to a large extent on how well you manage the communication process.

Let's Talk Frames

The term "frame of reference" refers to the lens by which you filter information that comes to you. The words you hear, the things you see are all processed and filtered through your frame of reference. You take the words you hear and turn those words into images reflected through your distinct filter. I can say the words "old tree" to seven different people, and these individuals will have seven different images in their minds of an old tree. The frame of reference filter is influenced by what you have been taught, what you have experienced, and what you believe to be true. This frame of reference, both individual and organizational, will affect the way we encode (send) and decode (receive) messages.

Overcoming Communication Barriers

As you can imagine there are many barriers in the communication process. Here are a few suggestions as how to overcome the most common barriers:

- *Seek to understand different frames of reference.*
  One of the largest barriers to great communication is everyone's desire to make sure they are heard and understood. Nothing restricts communication more than everyone talking at the same time. And your lips don't have to move for you to talk. You can talk in your mind. You think about what you are going to say in response to the person who is talking. Instead of talking first, why not try listening first. Look to understand what those with whom you are communicating may be trying to say. What is their agenda? What do they want to accomplish? What is their frame of reference in the discussion? When

you do this, you will find it much easier to encode a message that accomplishes both what you and the person you are communicating with desires.

- *Recognize cultural differences.* Develop a heightened level of sensitivity for those from different cultures than your own. Make sure you are inclusive. Do not assume that everyone understands and/or agrees with the traditional cultural communication behaviors you might take for granted.
- *Watch out for traditional spiritual language.* Watch the spiritual jargon. If you are speaking with an individual who understands and embraces that language, then using it is fine. But do not assume that everyone understands when you use traditional phrases of the church. Ask yourself if you could choose different words that provide a more positive image for this person and still communicate your message.
- *Speak to express and not to impress.* Be concise when you can and use words that everyone in the audience understands. Or at least explain the meaning of potentially misunderstood words. This will help everyone receive the full understanding of the discussion without feeling embarrassed for having to ask what a word means.
- *Avoid information overload.* Don't provide too much information over a short time period. Remember that people can only process so much information. It is better to have two or three meetings to disseminate the information instead of feeding it through a fire hose.
- *Avoid conflicting signals.* Make sure your words match your actions. Saying one thing and then doing another is a quick way to shut down

communication with all but the spiritually courageous in your circle.

- *Have an open door policy and mean it.* Be approachable. Let people know they can come to you and discuss whatever is on their minds. When they come to you, make sure you don't ridicule them or make them feel unwanted.

Say It Like You Mean It

Verbal communication is where most people put the majority of their focus when disseminating information. Verbal communication is important because much of how we are perceived is based on others' observation of how we speak. Here are a few tips to consider when you are communicating verbally:

- *Know what you want to say.* Have a well-thought-out plan before you begin to speak. If your message is important, then it is worth taking the time to prepare to say it correctly.
- *Consider the listener's point of view.* How will your audience respond to the information you are about to present? Take their response into consideration as you prepare your presentation. Make adjustments as needed.
- *Communicate from the simple to the complex.* One of the quickest ways to have your audience lose interest is to talk over their heads or to speak in terms they do not understand. If you have complicated information to share, always begin your presentation with information that everyone can grasp and then methodically build on this information one layer after the other. Do not make the assumption that because you

understand it, everyone around you does. Make it easy for your audience to keep up with your presentation.

- *Select your words carefully.* Use words that everyone in the audience can understand. Be careful of using jargon. While you don't want to necessarily dumb down your presentation, you want to make sure your communication is understood by the vast majority of your audience, whether that's three people or three thousand.
- *Enunciate clearly.* Enough said.
- *Be courteous and natural.* Be gracious in your words, and most important, don't try to be someone you are not. Just be yourself.
- *Repeat as needed to make sure you are understood.* The most important part of your presentation is that your audience understands your message. Be prepared to do what is necessary to make sure this goal is achieved.
- *Establish and maintain a high level of eye contact.* If your presentation or discussion is in a one-on-one setting, then try to pick one eye and always look into that one eye, preferably the one closest to you. This allows you to project the greatest level of confidence and trustworthiness. If the audience is significantly larger, try to occasionally pick an individual and look them directly in the eye as you make your presentation.
- *Watch your body language.* Keep an eye out for nervous ticks. Remember that your body sends up to 70 percent of the stimuli in the communication process.

- *Watch for verbal fillers like "umm", "err", "you know" and "uhh."* Practice until you can make your presentation with as few of these fillers as possible.
- *Don't be redundant.* Don't go over and over the same material as though you are speaking with a small child. Redundancy is insulting. Be sure to gauge your audience to understand how much repetition is too much.
- *Relax.* You are intelligent and prepared. You are competent and you are a nice person, and this will come across in your presentation when you relax. Loosen up. Everything will work out just fine.

The Pen Is Mightier Than the Sword

Written communication is a necessary part of almost any relationship or organization. The challenge with written communication is that you do not have the benefit of facial expressions, voice tone or inflection, or body language. Because of this, it is important to pay extra attention to the words you choose. Here are a few ideas to make your written communication a pleasure for those who receive it:

- *Clarity.* Go out of your way to make your point clear. Read the message and read it again. Read it from the point of view of the recipient. Is it possible they might have some questions or doubt? If so, do your best to eliminate it on the front end.
- *Concise.* Keep it short and to the point. Chances are your message is not the only one your recipient will receive that day.

- *Correct.* Make sure the information contained in your message is correct. Is it truthful? Is it proper? Would others approve?
- *Courteous.* Make the recipient feel comfortable and appreciated.
- *Condensed.* Do your best to avoid long, rambling sentences. They are difficult to read and can make it difficult for the reader to follow your thought process.
- *Avoid jargon.* You might know what your message means, but are you sure the recipient knows what all your words mean? If not, don't use them; seek words the reader can relate to.
- *Avoid trite phrases.* Get rid of corny, stale, tired, and overused clichés and phrases.

Body Talk

Scientists have determined that while verbal communication is important, up to 70 percent of face-to-face communication is accomplished through our body language. Nonverbal signals include eye contact, gestures, facial expressions, posture, body movements, and tone of voice. The question then becomes, "What is your body telling those you are communicating with?" Those with whom we communicate get the vast majority of their information from these nonverbals. With this being the case, it is significant that we spend some time focusing on our nonverbal communication. Be aware of the following potential nonverbal issues:

- *Have good eye contact.* Do your best to gain and maintain eye contact that shows that you are interested in the person in front of you and what

he or she has to say. Also maintain eye contact when that person is listening to you.
- *Concentrate on having your tone of voice reflect your true feelings.* If you are excited or empathetic, allow those emotions to come through in your tone. Be genuine in this process; your audience will know it if you are not.
- *Eliminate incongruent behavior.* As an example, don't say that you are sad with a smile on your face.

In Review

Communicating effectively is a simple and yet complicated endeavor. To become effective communicators, we must understand different frames of references (both others and our own), and put in place a personal process to help us overcome our natural barriers to effective communication.

Additionally, we should always consider the potential effects of our verbal, nonverbal, and written communication on those we are attempting to impact positively for Jesus Christ.

Live the life you want to live. Be the person you want to remember.

Chapter 5

Foster an Atmosphere of Open Communication

Nothing is more important to the success of a group or organization than communication. You can have people focused on the same goal. They can all agree on the process of how to achieve that goal. They can be talented and resourceful. But if they are unable to communicate effectively, and they don't operate within an atmosphere that leads to effective, open communication, this organization will never achieve success.

Therefore the process or system of communication within any group that desires to become successful is crucial. Disorganized or ineffective communication has a high potential to lead to failure. As a leader you must lead by example. If you desire to have a culture of effective communication, pay close attention to the elements that can indeed create the right atmosphere for the most effective, open communication possible.

Interact Openly and Honestly

As an example of positive communication, you must keep in mind the tips from chapter 4, but in addition to the tools for actually communicating a message, pay attention to the patterns of communication that you and your organization express. Look for ways to keep the channels open and honest between all members of your group, team, or organization. Here are some tips:

- *Make sure your communication is timely.* Don't wait two weeks to follow up on a conversation in writing. Don't wait until two hours before a meeting to send out the agenda. Timely communication shows that you care about the individual(s) you are communicating with, and it builds your reputation as a positive leader.

- *Again, be aware of nonverbal communication.* Have an awareness of what your nonverbal communication looks like and how it affects those around you, both one-on-one and in larger presentations. Don't be afraid to ask for feedback on your communication style.
- *Give positive constructive feedback.* Don't let all of your feedback be negative. Catch people doing a good job and compliment them. Let your feedback tell the story of your genuine concern and desire to help the individual grow and get better.
- *Sort out any vague messages.* Sometimes things sound good in our minds, but when we try to communicate them, the message becomes muddled. Communicate from the viewpoint of the individual you are trying to communicate with. If you were in their position, would you have trouble understanding your message? If so, make the necessary adjustments.
- *Get your point across succinctly.* Don't try to be unnecessarily cute or verbose. Be as concise as you can while still providing the information necessary to make your point clear.
- *Be direct but nonaggressive.* Sometimes people perceive someone who speaks directly to a situation as being aggressive. Be aware of that and form your direct comments in a way that removes the appearance of aggression, as much as you can.
- *Say what you think.* With as much love, humility, and grace as possible, tell others what you think is important. These comments must seek to lead to positive outcomes.

- *Don't put anyone down.* Focus on problems and not people. Everyone is of equal value. All must be allowed to maintain their dignity.

Deal Positively with Contrary Viewpoints

As leaders and team members both, we will often come into opposing or even conflicting viewpoints as you pursue goals and work toward the success of your group, organization, or ministry team. Part of creating an open communication atmosphere means learning how to deal with such contrary opinions in a positive, even constructive way. Use the following ideas to help avoid a negative confrontation over disagreements, and to keep things from escalating to a point of real conflict when possible:

- *Watch your verbal and nonverbal response.* Don't scowl or become impatient when confronted with viewpoints opposite of your own. You don't necessarily get to decide if your opinion is more important than someone else's. Be aware of your nonverbal communication as well as your words as you respond.
- *Wait until a person is done speaking.* Do not interrupt someone when they are speaking, even if you adamantly disagree. It is rude to arbitrarily cut someone short in midsentence. Don't interrupt others, and don't allow others to interrupt those in your group.
- *Ask for verification and clarification.* Don't allow others to make wild claims without specific proof. Claims that cannot be verified are not real claims at all and should be discarded. Ask additional clarifying questions if you or members of your

group do not have a clear understanding of the topic being discussed.

- *Look for areas of agreement.* Whenever we hear a contrary viewpoint, our first inclination is to bristle and to mentally begin preparing our rebuttal. Stop! Instead of being defensive, try to find areas where you agree. You may be surprised to find a synergy between the points of view that makes them both better. After you have looked for areas of agreement, then and only then specify points of disagreement and why you disagree. Make sure you can verify your viewpoint as well. The why behind the points of disagreement is the most important concern. Anyone can disagree. Knowing the whys will allow you to find common ground.

Provide Open Access to Information

As a leader, make sure your team members don't feel "in the dark" about communication they need to function in their roles effectively. While some information must be shared in the right time with the right people, keep the access to information as open as possible within your group, team, or organization. When people feel they are informed, they will have more buy-in to the vision and direction of the organization. The following ideas will keep information flowing openly:

- *Encourage people to identify the help they need and give them access.*
- *Share more information than necessary.* Too many leaders believe that controlling access to information makes them powerful. In fact, what it really does is make the organization weaker. When

people understand that you trust them with information, they usually respond positively.

- *Communicate your desire to provide open access.* Then actually provide open access as you determine necessary, to grow trust and an atmosphere of openness.
- *Make sure there are no surprises.* Get out in front of important situations in your communication process. Don't allow significant events to sneak up on your group without proper advance communication.
- *Route messages to all interested parties.* Make sure everyone who needs to be in the loop is actually in the loop.
- *Build relationships by sharing both negative and positive information.* Remember that you are not doing your team a favor by only giving them the good news. The bad news provides an opportunity to coach, to lead by example, and to prove to your team that you trust them to deal with the situation in a positive manner.

Listen

While we've touched on the importance of listening, this communication skill can never be overemphasized. Listening is a crucial aspect of communication. It can reduce potential misunderstanding, ensure that communication is flowing effectively in all directions, and help create the open atmosphere you seek for your team or organization. Learn how to improve your ability to listen by using the following approaches:

- *Listen to understand, not to talk or respond.* This is a big challenge. Our natural reaction as we listen to others talk is to begin to formulate what we are going to say next to them. Seek to stay completely in the moment with the individual who is talking. Listen in a way that you might truly comprehend how this person feels, so that you can identify more closely with his or her needs.

- *Listen to the total message.* Do not shut down when you hear something you do not like or that you disagree with. Focus so that you can grasp the totality of the message.
- *Use open-ended questions.* Do not use questions with a yes or no answer unless you have confirmation that you have a good understanding of what the individual is trying to communicate.
- *Use paraphrasing to increase and improve communication.* This is a great technique to make sure you and the person speaking are on the same page. The following is an example of paraphrasing: "So what you are saying is that 'Good communicators will communicate more frequently with greater effectiveness.' Is that right?" You simply repeat the key point of what you think you heard the person say.
- *Use summary statements.* This is another technique that helps you make sure you and the person you are speaking with are walking hand in hand down the road of good communication. It is as simple as making a statement that summarizes what you believe has been communicated. You can use a summary statement at any time during a communication event. You can use a summary statement whether one-on-one or in a group setting. You definitely want to use a summary statement at the end of a communication event to make sure all parties are moving forward positively together.

- *Do not interrupt.* If you are talking, you are not listening.
- *Listen willingly to disagreements.* Do not become defensive. Look for areas of commonality.
- *Use clarifying questions to make sure you understand what is being said.*

Follow These Guidelines for Open Communication

Creating an open atmosphere for effective communication is not all about the message itself. Many other factors enter in when we are either sending or receiving communication from one another. For an effective communication process, here are a few more tips:

- Promptly respond to phone calls, emails, texts, notes, or any communication. Nothing says, "I don't care" like taking three days to return a phone call or text message. And when you don't care, people stop communicating with you. Or worse, you get a bad reputation as it relates to communication. Make it your business to return all phone calls and messages within twenty-four hours.
- Focus on understanding others instead of formulating your response (hear, listen, understand, interpret, and respond). Assume that the person talking really has something important to say.
- Avoid interrupting others. As difficult as it may be, listen to what others have to say, fully and completely, in the moment of their communication.
- When talking with others on the phone, avoid sorting through mail or doing other work. If you don't focus, you will become distracted. When you become distracted, the person you are talking to will

notice. Nothing says, "I wish I wasn't talking to you" like reading your mail while on the phone.

- Do not put someone on speakerphone unless there is a conference call in your office. Speakerphones add a touch of the impersonal to an already less-than-personal communication activity—talking on the phone. If there is not a good reason to use it, keep the speakerphone turned off.
- When disagreeing with someone, summarize what you think his or her position is before responding with your point of view.
- Maintain good eye contact without staring.
- Attend to the feelings behind the words, as well as the content, of any message given or received. Usually the feelings are fueling the words. Address the feelings and then the words, and you will be known as a good communicator.
- Do not shoot the messenger of bad news. Remember to focus on problems and not people.
- Hold regular formal and informal staff meetings. The more often you communicate in different settings, the better you become at being a good communicator.
- Make a point of updating the appropriate people even when nothing has developed. This is simply continuing the habit of open communication.
- Ask yourself, "Who needs to know about this," and make sure they do.
- Look and be interested. When listening, lean in to show interest.
- Again, watch your body language.
- If you cannot keep a commitment, let the individual know as soon as you know.

- Reschedule a conversation if you cannot give it your undivided attention.
- Ask open-ended questions that bring out information (how, what, when, where, who, describe, explain).
- Understand how your efforts help others succeed and make sure you are providing the necessary communication to foster their success.
- Err on the side of too much communication instead of too little.
- Adapt your listening behaviors to ensure they are respectful of another's culture.

The Final Rundown

Make it your first priority to understand people, even those with opposing viewpoints. (You might be surprised by what you learn.) Then, as your second priority, make sure you are understood. This will greatly assist you in promoting an atmosphere where team members feel released to communicate in a way that greatly benefits you and your organization.

Live the life you want to live. Be the person you want to remember.

Chapter 6

Focus on the Team

No problem is insurmountable. With a little courage, teamwork, and determination a person can overcome almost anything.

B. Dodge

If you desire to be an excellent team leader, it is imperative that your focus remains on the welfare and well-being of the team. It is impossible for an organization to be successful long-term if there is a fundamental breakdown in the well-being of its organizational teams. For an organization to be healthy, its teams must also be healthy. For the teams to be healthy, the leadership and workings within each team must also be healthy. This chapter will help you to cultivate behaviors that allow you to become a healthy team member and team leader as you focus on the team. Here are a few ideas that have proven successful in a variety of settings.

Create an Environment Conducive to Teamwork

Although any organization must have a certain degree of structure to work effectively, both leaders and team members are responsible for the team's success. A leader should never take on alone the task of creating a team atmosphere, and members shouldn't rely upon the leader to do this for them. Any group or team will have a unique personality, depending upon the leaders involved, the number and diversity of team members, and the tasks of the team. Yet no matter the makeup of your team, the leader and the members are accountable for creating the right environment to give the entire team the best chance for succeeding in its assigned tasks. Follow these suggestions to create the best sense of "team" possible:

- Have very little hierarchy—the less the better.
- Cooperation vs. competition. Make sure your team has a culture of cooperation and not competition. You may be competing with individuals or groups outside of your team, but inside your team, there must be a spirit of helping each other.
- Provide necessary resources to win (information, people, etc.).
- Give individual team members the authority to act on team decisions. Once the team has made a decision, it is important that individuals within that team have the right to act on that decision as it relates to them and their role or responsibilities.
- Conduct appraisals of both team and individual performances. You can expect the best results on those things that you determine to measure or evaluate.
- Lead by example. If you have never done a task and are not willing to do it, do not ask anyone else to do it. This is one of the best ways to be an effective team leader and member.

Build Your Team Leadership Skills

Being a great leader is more than just having a lot of great followers. And every team member should be seeking to learn and grow in a way that will increase his or her own leadership capabilities. When the team is working together effectively and seeking to build team and individual skills, the goals and vision will become clearer and tasks completed more efficiently. Use the following ideas to give your team members opportunities to contribute to the organization or church's vision, and to grow into new leaders themselves:

- Define and familiarize your team with its mission and vision. Can you articulate your team's mission and vision without reading it from a sheet of paper? If not, shame on you. Can your team? If not, shame on you and them. You cannot expect your team to implement a mission and vision that they do not know.
- Don't allow yourself to become a "seagull" leader. This is the type of leader that shows up, makes a lot of noise, messes everything up, and then leaves the situation worse for having been there. Trust your people until they have proven themselves untrustworthy.
- Conduct team-building sessions. These should help build team skills, confidence, and a family atmosphere.
- Make sure you get input from all members to insure buy in.
- Define and clarify all roles and responsibilities. Everyone on the team should know what his or her role and responsibilities are. And not only that, they should also know how these fit into the big picture and bring about the overall mission and vision.
- Provide opportunity for members to negotiate their roles and relationships. Just because you've always done it one way doesn't mean it can't be improved. If team members want to discuss their roles and how they can improve, welcome these conversations.
- Allow the team to work out roles and responsibilities and report to you. *Empower.*

- Set performance goals, both individually and corporately. These goals should align with the overall mission and vision of the organization. The accomplishment of these goals should bring you one step closer to the realization of your organizational mission and vision.
- Ask others to evaluate team effectiveness (clarity of purpose, problem solving, communication, decision making, quality of work, conflict resolution).
- Help team members understand each other better and appreciate each other's differences.
- If the team moves inherently toward some kind of group identity, reinforce the commonality.

Value Everyone 's Work

Each member of a team is significant and has value to the team's purpose and to the team's total contribution to the organization's goals and vision. When members feel they are valued, they will be more effective in their roles and responsibilities and buy in to the team's missions. Be sure to follow these suggestions for building value among your team:

- Administrative, staff, core, and noncore personnel are all valuable. Some think some functions are more important. No one must be considered more important. All should be seen as having equal value.
- Eliminate symbols that make one group or team member more important.
- Offer verbal recognition of everyone's contributions both individually and in group settings.
- Include all levels of team members in as much planning as possible.

- Request input from the entire team; ask everyone. Don't become partial with one group over another.
- Become especially attentive to comments from less assertive members who aren't comfortable contributing in a group.

Encourage Team Interaction

Once you have established and reinforced a sense of value among team members, seek to keep all members working together by encouraging active interaction. When members are all involved and cooperating well, there should be no sense of any one person's role or responsibility being more important than another. Utilize these ideas in creating the right type of interaction:

- The leader talks to the group, the group talks with the leader, and the group talks with the group.
- Send out agendas in advance. This is a sign of respect for your team members. It gives them the opportunity to come prepared to give their input and to ask questions. This is also a sign that you are prepared.
- De-emphasize your leadership role in seating arrangements. Don't feel as though you have to sit at the head of the table at every meeting or at any meeting. Believe me, everyone knows who the leader is.
- Establish the norm of interaction. Invite team members to respond to each other's comments. Avoid interrupting others.
- Redirect comments inappropriately directed to you. Encourage the following of the chain of command while also empowering others in their areas of functional responsibility.

- Before team meetings, ask another team member to lead a discussion on particular points.

Increasing Team Interdependence

In addition to interacting well together, an effective team is also interdependent. If you have created an effective team environment, this interdependence should be a natural result of the trust your team members have in their leader and each other. To help improve interdependence:

- Develop synergy. *Synergy* means the combined effort of all your team members is greater than its individual parts. Seek to create this in your team in the following ways:
  o Foster belief in the interdependence of the team.
  o The team must see interdependence as a strength.
  o The team must believe that the team can accomplish more together.
- Look for viewpoints you can agree with and support. With trust, your team members will freely offer their ideas for the good of the team and the mission of the group. Seek these method of building this trust:
  o Balance offering your ideas with accepting others.
  o Strive for compromise.
  o Share the credit with others.
  o Support team decisions once they are made.

Involve Others in the Decision

Your team does not operate in a vacuum; it is part of a larger organizational mission and vision. At times it will be necessary to communicate and interact with other team leaders and even other entire teams to accomplish a goal for the larger group or church. When appropriate, use these guidelines:

- Involve those who should be involved:
  - In meetings, make sure you clarify the purpose of the meeting, give the big picture and ask for help.
  - Inform the team of the meeting plan.
  - Inform the team how decisions will affect those that are involved.
  - Have the team determine the next course of action, if possible.
- Determine *your* level of competition versus cooperation.
  - Are you pushing your own ideas, not compromising?
  - Are you withdrawing from the group (mentally/physically) because they are not accepting your ideas?
  - Are you creating a win/lose scenario?

Celebrate Team Success

When as a team leader you have put these team-improvement suggestions into practice, your team should experience success in meeting its goals as part of the organizational vision and mission. When success occurs, be sure to celebrate that with your team in these ways.

- Appreciate the team's contributions (tell them).
- Publically acknowledge good team performance.
- Let the team know that effort does make a difference.
- Share information relative to the team's performance.
- Organize social outings around successful project completion or other team successes.

**Ten Requirements for a Great Team Leader
Or How to Win and Retain the Respect of Your Team**

Regardless of your tenure as a team leader, there are some key principles you must use as a guide if you are going to be effective in a fundamental way. You must really believe that you have something of value to offer to those that you lead, and believe in the mission of the organization or group. Your purpose is to get things done through your team in a way that satisfies the short-term and long-term operational objectives of your organization. The most challenging part of your task as a leader is to get things done "through your team." Different people, by their very nature, bring different frames of references to every situation. People communicate in different ways. They can see the exact same thing, and not see the exact same thing. As a team leader you must be committed to helping your team overcome any individual and corporate spiritual barriers and reach the God-ordained goals for their lives.

1. *Care about your people.* It is imperative that your team knows you genuinely care about them as individuals, and not just for the level of performance they can provide you or the organization. They must know they have a positive worth to you individually, independent of who they

are as ministry workers. Everyone is defined by more than the tasks they perform. Everyone has families and responsibilities outside of ministry work. Make it clear through your actions that you see them as more than an asset to the team. You must sincerely have a personal concern for each individual who is part of your team. People can determine whether you are sincere or not, and they will respond accordingly. This does not, however, mean that you substitute the standards of the organization, or your standards, for the standards of those on your team. It simply means that you must develop discernment for each situation that allows you to say: (1) "I care about you and understand that you may have pressures and responsibilities outside of the team environment, and I am sensitive to them," and (2) "The objectives of the organization, the team, and your area of responsibility still need to get done." Your ability to effectively balance these two potentially competing sentiments will go a long way in proving to your team that you are caring and sensitive, but also an effective leader.

2. *Maintain your position as leader, first.* New ministry leaders usually come from the rank of their peers. Many times new ministry leaders are now leading close personal friends. It is significant that as a leader, whether of your friends or not, you establish yourself as the leader first, instead of being a friend first. Don't get me wrong. As a ministry leader and a pastor, some of my best, closest, and dearest friends were those who served with me. However, there can never be a point in time when I cease to be viewed as their leader in the

ministry environment. You are the leader and ultimately responsible for the performance of the team. A friend may *choose* to be honest and tell friends when they are wrong. A leader has an *obligation* to be honest and tell team members when they have areas that need improvement, as they are led by the Holy Spirit and God's Word.

3. *Maintain high standards of excellence.* Don't allow situations or people to lower your standards of excellence, as revealed by the Word of God and the Holy Spirit. Make sure your words have power. This will happen as you maintain high standards. Be careful what you call "great" or "excellent." When someone does his or her job, it's not great. It might be good, but it's definitely not great. *Exceeding* expectations is great, and anything less than that is good, at best. Everything isn't *awesome.* Additionally, don't buy into the idea that somehow not meeting and exceeding the team's goals is acceptable. It's not! Some might try to convince you that because of conditions or unusual circumstances, missing your goals is tolerable. Don't get into the habit of making such excuses. Get into the habit of accomplishing goals and holding yourself and others accountable. Set the standard of excellence that says, "When we aren't meeting and exceeding goals, we are not performing at a level that is acceptable—period. Our team purpose is to always, always, always hit the goal we have been given."

4. *Don't avoid conflict.* In any relationship there will be conflict. The nature of relationships often leads to misunderstandings. One person wants one thing

and another wants something completely different. To think you can avoid conflict in any area of your life is naïve at best and spiritually unconscious at worst. The key to dealing positively with conflict is knowing which battles to engage in and which battles to ignore. The color of your team member's organizational folder is most likely a conflict you can ignore. The fact that a team member isn't following your direction in ministry duties, and as a result key goals have been missed, is something you cannot ignore. The key to handling conflict on your team is to do it as quickly as is appropriate, and have it come from a place that says, "I genuinely care for you, and the purpose of this conversation is to help you." If you really have that perspective, it will come through and make the conversation easier. The tension and anxiety that usually accompanies conflict won't magically disappear. However, you will get through the process with a greater sense of positive purpose, knowing that your motives are pure and you are doing the right thing for the right reason. My experience has proven that many times, out of the greatest conflict, the greatest successes are born. Additionally, without some level of conflict it is almost impossible to accomplish anything really great.

5. *Build a sense of team, a sense of family.* Help your team members genuinely care about each other. Give team members a little time at scheduled team meetings to talk about their families and the things that are important to them outside of ministry. When appropriate, celebrate accomplishments within your team that are not necessarily ministry related. Participate in special outings or events just

for your team. Look to build stories of fun and laughter that are specific to your team alone. Shout every team success, both individually and as a team. Make your team the best place within the organization.

6. *Be proactive—catch situations before they become a problem.* As you observe your team and notice areas that could become problems, work quickly to investigate the situation. Then address any problem areas immediately. When dealing with the situation, always seek to first understand the problem (it may not be what you think it is) and then try to help. Do not come in saying you know everything. You are not there to point out any team member's incompetence in allowing this situation to occur. Instead, approach the situation with the attitude that you see a potential problem, and that before making final judgment you want to make sure you understand the full scope of the situation from the team member's perspective. Ultimately, if there is a problem, your purpose is to help the individual handle it productively.

7. *Utilize the strengths of your top performers.* This is an area that can pay high dividends for all involved. Use your top performers to take some of the ministry weight from your shoulders. Usually they are willing to be utilized to a greater degree. Additionally, develop partnerships and accountability within your team by pairing a top performer with a low performer to allow the latter to see how a task or ministry goal should be done.

8. *Fight for your people.* Don't be afraid to stand up for your people. When they deserve something of significance, or don't deserve something that might be coming to them, make sure you are one of the first voices to stand and fight for what you know is right. If one of your people deserves recognition or special attention, make sure the appropriate people are aware of the situation.

9. *Allocate your time with your team members based on potential and openness to being coached.* Don't spend a majority of your time with the top performers. Typically, these individuals have got it figured out and only need an occasional tweak to keep it going in the right direction. Also, don't spend the majority of your time with the low performers, unless they have a high level of potential and are coachable. Spend the majority of your time with those members that are coachable and have a positive upside. What I mean by coachable is that they are not only willing to understand what they should do differently and to buy in to a different process but also that they quickly implement any changes. Spend your time with these team members, because this is where big gains are found.

10. *Regularly spend time with your team members.* In light of the above, set aside a certain amount of time on a regular basis to spend with each team member. Some members you might meet with weekly, some monthly, and some even quarterly, depending on their specific needs. Either way, use this time to observe, coach, understand, encourage, hold accountable, and follow up. Each meeting should

not be an entity unto itself, but should pick up from the last meeting and build positively upon it. This will ensure that each member is on track, progressing along the path you have mutually agreed upon, and will reduce misunderstandings along the way.

Maximize Your Performance by Focusing on the Following

As you seek to focus on your team, here are a few other ideas to help keep your focus in the right place and create a successful and efficient team for your organization.

- Schedule an annual retreat to build team spirit.
- Know each member's strengths and limitations and make a plan to utilize the strengths.
- Avoid premature judging of others ideas.
- Pull your team together as a group to solve problems.
- Have fun.

I Want to Get Better

Take a look at the Team Progress Checklist in appendix C. Whether you are a team member or team leader, you can use this checklist to begin to evaluate if you are seeking to help your team learn to be as effective as possible.

Live the life you want to live. Be the person you want to remember.

Chapter 7

Become a Great Team Member

Good followers have the potential to become good leaders. If someone is not a good follower, it is almost impossible to become a good leader. No matter who you are, you are on someone's team. Most of us are followers in one area of our lives and leaders in another. In this chapter you will find ideas to help you become an excellent follower and an excellent leader. The teams we serve on need both.

Ten Ways to Become an Excellent Team Member

Everyone wants to do well. Everyone wants to be esteemed. Everyone wants to be viewed as an exceptional performer. However, experience shows that everyone is not willing to put forth the effort required to accomplish these goals. Quality team leaders look for specific characteristics in individuals to determine whether they might make excellent team members. Obviously, some basic foundational qualities are required—team members must remain organized, arrive on time, and meet the standard of their current responsibilities. Assuming that you meet these basic qualities and are functioning as a solid team member in the requirements of your current role, now you can consider what you might do differently to move forward to the next level in your ministry. You should seek a greater calling, a higher level of service to Christ. You should want to move from good to better, and from better to best. The following ten ideas will help you move forward into excellence on your team and beyond simply meeting your team responsibilities.

   The enclosed list is merely that, one list, and is in no way exhaustive. However, they are some of the most important, impactful steps you can make today. If and when you implement these ten ideas and make them a part of your daily routine, you likely will witness positive change in your professional, spiritual, and personal life. Here are ten ways to become an excellent team member—beginning today.

1. *Be a "go to" and "get it done" team member.* Develop a reputation within your work unit of being the individual who always "gets it done" on time, within budget, and with the desired results. Do not make excuses about why things don't get done. If you do not make excuses, you will not be tempted to rely on excuses. Nobody cares about all the storms you encountered; they simply want to know if you got the job done. Understand with whom you need positive relationships to get things done, and then develop those relationships. Team leaders love nothing more when rolling out a new program or implementing a change, than knowing they do not have to worry about John or Jane. Why? Because John and Jane will get it done and get it done right. When you become this type of "go to" team member, you have the reputation of being a winner, and everyone wants a winner on their team.

2. *Focus on positive outcomes.* Too many times I have seen team members erroneously believe that activity equals production. Don't be deceived. Activity simply means work, and unfocused work is a waste of time and energy. Focus on results and the activities that produce those desired results. Don't spend time running in circles for the sake of being busy. No one cares. Be persistent in your focus. Don't let others tell you it's alright that you didn't

get the required results—it's not. There may be legitimate reasons why you didn't get the results you needed, and you can learn from those situations. But do not fall asleep and begin to think that great effort justifies subpar results—it doesn't. Stay focused on excellent outcomes and be satisfied with nothing less.

3. *Focus on the positive and not the negative. Become a positive leader through change and adversity.* The one thing that organizations never have enough of is positive leadership. As a society, we have a natural tendency to spend more time on what is wrong versus what is right. Ten things might well be perfect and one thing a little askew, and most people will spend the majority of their time talking about the one thing that is wrong versus the ten things that are right. This lends itself to the "water cooler" experience and the "grapevine" phenomenon, where team members find the time to commiserate with each other about all that is wrong in their world. The chatter increases significantly during organizational change and adversity. Your ability to focus on the positive in the midst of adversity shows you are a strong team member and leader. You should acknowledge the reality of the situation; life presents us with many challenging conditions. If you are unwilling to honestly recognize the difficulties that situations present, it will paint you as naïve at best and inconsiderate and uncaring at worst. So admit the challenges. Acknowledge the adversity. Concede the difficulty that each situation offers—but don't live there. Don't sit down in the desert of your opportunity. Get up and move forward. Focus on the ten things

that are right. Focus on the ten reasons why this can and will work. Focus on the ten things you can do to make the situation better long-term. Remember, the only reason adversity shows up is to mock your commitment to excellence. Keep your attention on the positive, not blindly but boldly. You will prove that you represent the rare team member they are all looking for—a positive leader.

4. *Display passion, dedication and an unambiguous intention.* First, let others see your passion for your role. This is demonstrated not by having a giant grin painted on your face all the time like a clown, but much more so in your behavior. Enthusiasm is demonstrated in your preparedness for all areas of your role. Are you at meetings early? Are you willing to enthusiastically stay late or come in early to work on special projects (you don't *have* to be there—you *get* to)? Are you willing to proactively help others? Second, dedication is shown in your loyalty to the organization, your perseverance during difficult times, your willingness to be there when needed, and your willingness to support the organization when you may not agree with or understand completely all the actions you see them taking. Third, is it obvious you are there to provide excellent results? Is everyone clear that you are following direction and have a great desire to help the organization meet its short-term and long-term objectives?

5. *Demonstrate continuous personal improvement.* Personal improvement is your responsibility alone. The organization may have an interest in your development, but ultimately this falls squarely and

permanently at your feet. No matter who you are, and no matter what position you hold, you can always improve. Set a goal of personal development, whether on a daily, weekly, or monthly basis. Take a class, read another book, listen to a CD, subscribe to a magazine—the list goes on. But whatever you do, don't lie to yourself and believe you have everything you need to continue to function at a high level and help move your organization forward. Don't think you don't have to get better, that you have arrived. That mind-set is a prescription for moving from being a hero to being a has been. Developing a mind-set of continuous improvement will keep you sharp; it will let you know where you are vulnerable and allow you the opportunity to do something positive about it. Remember, the game is always changing, so if you don't want to lose your spot or be left behind, you must continually improve your skill set and competencies.

6. *Do more than is expected.* Whatever your role requirements and functional area, make sure you do more than the minimum requirements of your position. Don't look to just get by. In fact, take a close look at the position you would like to be elevated to, and begin to function in your current role, as best you can, as though you were already functioning in that next-level role. Do it with enthusiasm and without any timetable of expectation.

7. *Understand the key focuses of the organization and make sure you contribute to those areas as you carry out your responsibilities.* Different

organizations have different ideas about what is significant to their long-term success. I have worked with various establishments who considered computer skills, positive leadership, decision making, and/or innovation as significant to their long-term success. Your organization is probably completely different, and that is fine. What is important is to identify within your company's long-term strategies the area(s) where you as a team member can contribute. As you contribute, begin to verbalize this contribution as part of your interaction with your team leadership and peers— not to boast but to demonstrate alignment and commitment to the organization's goals and to encourage others to do the same. This is leadership by example. It is vital that you begin to internalize these strategies so that you can "talk the talk" as you "walk the walk." Additionally and most important, you must move forward and begin to implement a personal strategy of demonstrating that you are able to have positive impact for the organization in these areas.

8. *Share your ministry goals with your team leader.* You might think this one goes without saying, but nothing important goes without saying. Be clear. Let them know what you're willing to do and what you are not. Do not wait for your team leader to originate these discussions.

9. *Look for additional challenges.* Network the organization and begin to understand where there might be opportunities for you to take on additional responsibility. This might mean a special project or

a special committee. Always look to funnel these requests through your team leader if appropriate.

10. *Take on a role in another area of the organization.* No matter what functional area you are working in, consider taking a position in a different area of the organization. This will accomplish several positive things. It will give you invaluable experience in a different area of the organization. It will broaden your horizons about the organization and what is required to become successful. It will make you more valuable to the team. Finally, it will prove your commitment to the organization and your commitment to your personal continuous improvement.

Increase Your Effectiveness

As you seek to be the best possible team member, and even grow into an effective leader, here are a few more ideas to keep your focus in the right place and for the right purpose:

- Check your ego at the door. This is about Christ and the Kingdom agenda. It's not about you, your church, your pastor, your friends, or your problems.
- Stay focused on the mission. Honor God, build up the church, and win souls for Christ.
- Focus on what you can do to make things better; stay in harmony with the will and Word of Christ.
- Be less judgmental of others. Focus on people's good qualities.
- Check your common courtesies (greet people, say please and thank you).

- Apologize to those you have hurt or ignored. When was the last time you said, "I'm sorry"? If you can't remember, it has definitely been too long.
- Extend yourself to others. Get to know them outside of church.
- Be more tolerant of others. Don't think of yourself as better or more important than others. Take the time to respect others and their opinions.
- Don't take people for granted. Have a genuine interest. Seek to understand and know about others by showing interest in their families and personal lives.
- Smile more. It's easy. Try it today.
- Don't be sarcastic. Don't use a wry sense of humor as a way to tease, mock, or be cute. Not everyone is going to get it. Those that do not get it will think you are a jerk.
- Be friendly, positive, and optimistic. Always expect to see the best in others. Always believe in a positive outcome. A positive attitude is contagious.
- Compliment others. Look for the opportunity to catch people doing something well and compliment them on it.
- Look to help others without being asked. It's nice to react to a request for help with positive response, but significantly more gracious to react to someone's need proactively, without being asked. When you see someone in need, make it your responsibility to help him or her as much as you can, as quickly as you can. Don't allow yourself to become so self-centered or busy that you fail to notice the needs and concerns of others.
- Do not use your position or information to take advantage of others.

- Provide a positive surprise. Look for opportunities to make people smile.
- Always look to increase your self-awareness and emotional intelligence.

Live the life you want to live. Be the person you want to remember.

Chapter 8

Value Diversity

What is diversity? Diversity is not simply having people around us with a different skin color or a different culture—it's much more. Diversity is our willingness to be open-minded about those unlike us. The spirit of diversity concludes that we should go out of our way to include those who would not otherwise be included. Diversity is in effect the heart of Jesus Christ. It is God's will because He wants us to find unity in Him in diversity. This sends a compelling message into the world about the power of Jesus Christ. We must understand that there is strength and synergy in true diversity. We must value diversity, according to God's Word.

God's View of Diversity

God loves and has great value for diversity. All we have to do is to take a look at creation. The variety that we find in nature is stunning. Even as we look at the color and cultures of humankind, the diversity God created is astonishing. It is obvious that God not only enjoys diversity but He also values it.

> *For he [Christ] himself is our peace, who has made the two groups one and has destroyed the barrier, the dividing wall of hostility.*
> Ephesians 2:14

What the Creator meant for our good (variety and diversity), the enemy has used against us to thwart the purpose of God. We have allowed God's divinely ordained diversity to become a barrier between us and those who are not like us. Christ never meant for people of different races to worship separately. He never desired that there be division between the rich and poor. He never meant for there to be any divisions, instead He died to remove them. We have erected man-made barriers God never intended to exist. Yet now we have become comfortable worshiping our gods of tradition, comfort, convenience, and predictability. This is not the heart of Jesus Christ.

> *I urge you, brothers and sisters, to watch out for those who cause divisions and put obstacles in your way that are contrary to the teaching you have learned. Keep away from them. For such people are not serving our Lord Jesus Christ, but their own appetites.*
> Romans 16:17–18

Thank God for Jesus! Christ Jesus specializes in tearing down man-made walls and barriers, all of which should have never been erected. Christ has torn down the wall between sinful man and a holy God. He has torn down the wall between the Jew and the Greek. He has torn down the wall between the races, between rich and poor, and every other man-made wall. He has torn down these walls because they never should have existed. He has torn down these walls because if left erected they are barriers that hinder the accomplishment of the gospel here on earth. Christ has torn down the walls because when we live a life of integration and diversity, it brings Him great honor and glory. When we live these God-ordained lives of diversity and variety, it proves to the world the authentic power of Jesus Christ. Without His power, the life of authentic diversity, in love and in harmony, would be impossible.

*I appeal to you, brothers and sisters, in the
name of our Lord Jesus Christ, that all of
you agree with one another in what you say
and that there be no divisions among you,
but that you be perfectly united in mind and
thought.*

1 Corinthians 1:10

Diversity Is an Important Positive

If diversity is important to God and He views it as positive
for His glory, then we should do the same. How boring it
would be if we were always surrounded by people who
looked like us, thought like us, and agreed with us. Not
only would it be boring but it would also be dangerous,
because we would all have the same blind spots and
weaknesses. In the church we should find diversity in color,
diversity in culture, diversity in gifts, and diversity in
process, but never diversity in purpose. Through diversity
we are actually made stronger as we use our God-ordained
differences to look out for each other and provide each
other with different perspectives that provide growth and
direction. We honor God, and we are better and stronger,
when we embrace those who are not like us. This
represents the heart of Jesus Christ.

Steps to Increase Your Team's Diversity

As you either lead or participate in your organizational team, look for signs within yourself and your team of attitudes that do not embrace diversity. The following suggestions will help you and your team become more aware of the attitudes and behaviors that need to change if you are to express the heart of Jesus Christ through diversity in your organization, group, or church:

- Search your automatic thoughts and language for unexamined assumptions and stereotypical responses.
- Challenge yourself and others about prejudiced behavior or comments. Allow opportunity to change without penalty.
- Watch for any tendencies to joke about differences. Are they really jokes? Or are they your prejudices coming to the surface?
- Stand up and speak out when others aren't valued or their ideas not considered.
- Challenge organizational policies that might be exclusionary or assumptions that limit opportunity.
- Become a mentor to an individual whose background and experiences are different than yours.
- Make sure groups are diverse when developing opportunities or looking for answers to problems.
- Give feedback to others whose different beliefs and actions negatively affect their credibility and effectiveness. Be open and honest, but also respectful.

Please Encourage Me

God values diversity. We should value what God values. We are encouraged by Christ Himself to discard our gods of tradition, pride, prejudice, preference, comfort, convenience, and predictability. If we are true disciples of Jesus Christ, we must go out of our way to include those who don't look or act like us. Is this not the spirit of Christmas? Is this not the spirit of the cross?

To help you begin to challenge your thought process regarding diversity, take a look at appendix D. Complete the two exercises you find there. As you complete each one, evaluate why you feel and think as you do regarding each specific area of both exercises. Are your feelings and thoughts honoring Christ?

Live the life you want to live. Be the person you want to remember.

Chapter 9

Learn to Effectively Handle Conflict

Conflict makes us uncomfortable, so many people avoid it at all cost. However, whenever we are involved in any type of relationship, there will be conflict. It is inevitable and unavoidable. The question is not whether we are going to deal with conflict but how we will handle the conflict. We are going to be offended. How we deal with the offense will determine much of our effectiveness as leaders.

Conflict—the Foundation of a Great Relationship?

We must change our perspective about conflict. We must no longer see it as a negative, something to be avoided. We must begin to see conflict as a positive opportunity to build stronger and deeper relationships.

The best thing we can do in this area is to not become easily offended. We are easily offended when we think too highly of ourselves, when we take ourselves too seriously. At times we are overly concerned about our honor instead of being concerned about honoring Jesus Christ. We want to make sure that our position and power are recognized, instead of recognizing God's position and power. We are focused on making sure we get recognition for what we have done, instead of putting the focus on what Christ has done.

We must have confidence in our position in Jesus Christ if we are to become humble servants of God. When we are confident of our position in Him, we do not have to be honored by humans, because we have already been honored by God. Our confidence in our position in Christ produces security in our relationship with Him. This security produces humility, which allows me to overlook small insignificant things that might offend others.

If we cannot overlook the offense, the Word of God encourages us to confront the individual in a one-on-one situation. Undoubtedly this is one of the most challenging things to do, to tell someone he or she has done something to offend you. It is equally difficult to tell someone that an offense committed was not only wrong but also did not provide a positive testimony about Jesus Christ. When these situations are handled appropriately, they can provide an opportunity for sincere growth both spiritually and relationally. Here are a few thoughts to consider:

1. We only have the right to find offense in those things that would offend Jesus Christ. If we cannot find biblical evidence that something offends God, we should get over it. Don't confront people about your preferences or their process for doing something. Don't major in the minors. Don't get upset about things that ultimately are insignificant. Don't confront someone about how you feel. Don't confront someone over opinions. The foundation of your offense must remain biblical. If not, pray and ask God to help you to grow spiritually to a place where these types of issues are not a problem for you.

2. Go to the individual as soon as you can. Do not wait, but do not go in haste. Do not confront in anger. Make sure you bathe the situation in prayer and ask Christ to give you a heart of grace and compassion. But do not put this conversation off indefinitely. It must get done sooner rather than later.

3. The confrontation must remain in love and humility with much grace. Remember that many times

people do not know they have offended you. Use a "sandwich" approach in your discussions. Start by telling the individual about some of the things that you genuinely admire about him or her. After having done that, graciously, humbly, and lovingly talk about the area of your offense. Keep the conversation Bible focused. Discuss the situation and get the person's feedback. After this discussion, be quick to reaffirm the individual and his or her positive traits.

4. If someone comes to you that you have offended, do your best not to be defensive. The fact that this person is having this conversation with you, in love and humility, proves that he or she loves Jesus and loves you. Of all the things this person could do today, having this conversation with you is most certainly at the bottom of the list.

5. Do not be overly critical. Focus on the problem and not the person. Speak pleasant words. Do not let the conversation focus on opinions. The conversation must center on the Word of God. Be gracious with others the way Christ has been gracious with you.

6. Do not overreact. Make your point and move forward. Allow the individual to leave the conversation with dignity, even if unable to agree to make a change or see things your way.

7. Never confront anyone for your own motives or for revenge. We only have the right to confront when the purpose of our intervention is the betterment of the person we are confronting.

A word fitly spoken is like apples of gold in settings of silver.
                              Proverbs 25:11, NKJV

Small Foxes Destroy the Vine

Whoever said, "The devil is in the details," told the truth. The devil shows up in the small things. The big things usually have a way of getting done and taking care of themselves. In the small things we find the most division and conflict.

We are challenged to be mindful of the fact that as believers we are all one. We are the same. We are part of the body of Christ. Just as your finger is different than your toe, yet is the same, so are we as believers. We are to be mindful to not think more highly of ourselves than we do of others. For when we believe that our opinions are more valuable than others, we find ourselves defending what ultimately is irrelevant. It's nice to have an opinion, but what we really need to know is not what we think, but what does God's Word say about it. We must remember that God's desire for us is that we have no division. Meditate on that idea for a moment. No division based on denomination, race, culture, socioeconomic status, etc.—no division.

> *But God has put the body together, giving greater honor to the parts that lacked it, so that there should be no division in the body, but that its parts should have equal concern for each other. If one part suffers, every part suffers with it; if one part is honored, every part rejoices with it. Now you are the body of Christ, and each one of you is a part of it."*
> 1 Corinthians 12:24–27

Our Pride, Our Preference, and Our Prejudice

Whenever people come together, we have the opportunity for conflict and offense. God tells us that He is a God of differences. He takes things and people that are completely different, and as they submit to His power and authority, He uses them to do great things in the Kingdom of God. In fact, He prefers to use things that don't necessarily go together because it brings more attention, honor, and glory to Him. He specializes in bringing the Jew and the Greek together, the slave and the free, the rich and the poor, the black and the white—all for His glory.

For we were all baptized by one Spirit so as to form one body—whether Jews or Greeks, slave or free—and we were all given the one Spirit to drink.
1 Corinthians 12:13

There are different kinds of gifts, but the same Spirit distributes them. There are different kinds of service, but the same Lord. There are different kinds of working, but in all of them and in everyone it is the same God at work. . . . Just as a body, though one, has many parts, but all its many parts form one body, so it is with Christ.
1 Corinthians 12:4–6, 12

In the above scripture passages, Paul tells the church at Corinth, and us as well, that God takes our differences and orchestrates them divinely and supernaturally to accomplish the mission of the gospel. We are different in our individual temperaments. We are different in our spiritual gifts, and therefore we are differently equipped to provide spiritual service. And these differences in our ability to provide spiritual service provide different kinds of work each of us is equipped to do. But God takes all of these differences, all of these parts, and uses them to effectively and productively form the body of Christ. There is a great supernatural release when the body of Christ is working together as orchestrated by the Holy Spirit, with everyone being productive in the area of their giftedness. This supernatural release of power accomplishes the mission of Christ on earth that the spirit of offense seeks to destroy.

The establishment of all nonbiblical offense is based upon our pride, our preference, and our prejudice. Our pride—our self-importance, our arrogance—propels us to make sure that we are satisfied, honored, and esteemed. Our preference values our opinions over the opinions of others and builds an inherent hierarchy of favoritism. Our prejudice—our bias, our preconceptions—shows our intolerance for others who are different from us in any way. We must consciously throw aside our pride, preference, and prejudice and pick up the concept of *oneness*. This is pleasing to God. This focuses us to make sure that God is satisfied, honored, and esteemed. The concept of *oneness* in Jesus helps us esteem others above ourselves and tears down the wall of favoritism, as we begin to understand that no one person is more valuable than another.

There are many ways to clean a house. Someone might start in the bedrooms and someone else might start in the basement. What is significant is not the process of cleaning the house. It is not how I cleaned the house. What is significant, and what we should stay focused upon, is that the house was adequately cleaned. If the answer is yes, then move forward.

God calls us to unity in diversity and unity of purpose. He does not call us to unity in process. Our pride, preferences, and prejudice are doors for evil that hinder us from seeing the big picture of who God is and what His desire is for us as members of the church universal. Keep in mind that God is more focused on purpose than on process. We all might agree on a purpose and then have a *knock-down, drag-out fight* over the process. Do not fight about the way something gets done as long as it gets done and the process does not dishonor God. If you can internalize this thought process, it will prevent many offenses and conflicts.

Internal Service Contracting

"Internal service contracting" is a preventative action we can take to prevent conflict. This includes understanding who your internal customers are. A customer is anyone for whom you provide information or services as part of your team role. A team member may be seen as an internal customer. This means you must understand who needs information or services from you. Write down their names and the information or services they need from you, then schedule a dialogue with each individual internal customer in order to ascertain the following:

- What is the information or service these customers need you to provide?
- How often do they need you to provide this information or service?
- How do your internal customers determine success?
- If you are unable to provide the information or service, how will this affect them and the services they provide?
- What else do they need from you to do their jobs with excellence?

The purpose of this dialogue is to come away with a documented understanding and agreement about how each customer can meet the explicit needs and requirements of the other, in a way that both can perform their duties with excellence.

The Stages of Conflict

Conflict occurs in several stages. A good leader can spot the early stages and intervene preemptively. The best outcome to conflict is to avoid it completely, if possible. The next best outcome is to resolve conflict as quickly and effectively as possible. The stages to conflict are as follows:

1. People want something and someone keeps them from having it. They want something specific, whether an object or their preference.
2. Then they explain or express frustration by blaming someone they feel is responsible. They potentially retaliate against the party they feel prevented them from having what they wanted. Both parties feel frustrated.
3. Both parties then react out of frustration, and conflict escalates.
4. The leader sees the situation getting out of hand.
5. The good leader acts on the opportunity for resolution and the development of a stronger relationship moving forward, if handled appropriately.

Ways to Manage Conflict

There are several alternative ways to deal with conflict, depending on the situation, the level of conflict, and the position of the parties involved. Here are a few ideas:

1. *Exercise dominance or force.* This method can be used if you are in need of a quick decision or if an unpopular action needs to be taken. You must be in a position of authority to take this approach. You must be direct without being overly aggressive.

2. *Give in.* This method of conflict management is appropriate when you are wrong or if the issue is more significant to others than to you. This method builds strong relationships as well as "social credit." It also can provide a higher level and sense of synergy within the group or organization.

3. *Compromise.* This method is always useful, especially when the parties involved are of equal power and have mutually exclusive goals.

4. *Avoid or postpone.* If the issue is trivial, if there are more important pressing issues, or if people need to cool down, this method of conflict management is suggested.

5. *Gain a different perspective.* It is always recommended in a conflict situation to take the time and make the effort to try to understand the position of the other individual(s). Try to see the state of affairs from the opponent's perspective.

6. *Collaborate for a win-win.* This is always the correct method to use when: (a) all concerns are too

important to compromise, (b) strong feelings must be worked out, and (c) you are looking to gain long-term commitment through genuine consensus.

A Model for Conflict Resolution

There is a model we can use to resolve conflict. This process allows you to get to the real issues and provide clear resolutions for all involved.

- *Listen*—allow venting. Do not raise your voice even though the other party might be yelling. Allow the individual to vent until he or she has calmed down. Keep asking the question, "Is there anything else?" Do not move forward until the individual is calm and has gotten all complaints and emotions out in the open.
- *Share*—that you heard and understood. Repeat back what you heard the person say to make sure you are both on the same page.
- *Clarify*—restate the problem as a question. In this moment you take all of the information the individual has given you and state what you believe is the real problem, but do so in the form of a question. An example is to say, "So what I hear you really saying is that you are unhappy with the service we have given you over the last thirty days. Is that correct?" If your restatement of the problem is incorrect, make sure to ask additional clarifying questions until you feel as though you have a clear understanding of the situation. Restate the problem again as a question. Continue in this manner until the two of you agree that you have accurately restated the problem. This agreement is your signal to move on to the next step.

- *Present*—answers in terms of ideas or options. Provide a dialogue that seeks to present an acceptable answer or resolution to the complaint. Do not feel as though you have to come up with this answer alone. You can and should ask the individual for input as to how the problem can be resolved, understanding that any recommendation might lean toward the extreme.
- *Ask*—for action on a positive solution. Once you have what is considered a viable solution to the problem, ask for specific and measurable action on behalf of all parties, to secure a resolution.

Effectively Handle Conflict

As you follow the suggestions in this chapter when conflict arises between you and another individual on your team, or in your organization or group, you will help bring harmony and resolution to the situation. As a result, your team will be more effective, and you will improve your own leadership skills. Keep the following additional principles in mind whenever conflict threatens the unity of your team:

- Bring conflict out into the open.
- Listen first to understand the opposing viewpoint prior to articulating your own.
- Approach conflict situations as an opportunity to strengthen interpersonal relationships.
- At the beginning of a conflict discussion, express your desire for a resolution that benefits all involved.
- Encourage others to depersonalize the conflict.
- Listen to understand and not to respond.
- Do not lecture about why you are right and others are wrong; simply state your point of view.

- Clearly articulate the points of agreement prior to dealing with the points of disagreement.
- Attack problems not people.
- Value people and not things.
- Seek communication not frustration.
- Remember that if an issue is significant, it must be confronted.
- Don't push aside significant issues to the detriment of the mission of the team or organization. If you cannot get past an issue, it must e confronted.

Help Me Handle It

This is most likely the area in which you will have the greatest challenge as a team leader or member. For most of us, our natural desire to avoid conflict only postpones the inevitable, and in doing so increases the intensity of the encounter.

Seek to change your perception of conflict. Begin to see conflict as a potential positive, which if handled properly, and if handled biblically, can bring benefit, harmony, and resolution, and make the team more effective.

Take a look at the case study in appendix E. After reviewing the story, make a list of areas where things went wrong in the encounter. Make a note to avoid these pitfalls in your current and future positions. Additionally, in the case study, determine the necessary steps the parties should take to move things forward positively. Then think about how you could take the same steps in resolving conflict in your own team or in a particular situation you may face. Take some time to discuss your findings with a mentor or close friend.

Live the life you want to live. Be the person you want to remember.

Chapter 10

Walk the Talk

*Therefore, I urge you, brothers, in view of
God's mercy, to offer your bodies as living
sacrifices, holy and pleasing to God – this is
your spiritual act of worship.*

Romans 12:1

There is not much in our lives that we can control. We
cannot control who our parents are, or the country we were
born in. Even as we drive down the road, we cannot control
whether we will arrive safely at our destination. When we
really stop and think about it, there is little in life that we
can control.

While we may not be able to orchestrate the events
of our lives, one thing we can control is how we react to
those events. We can control our attitudes. Our
encouragement is to have the perspective of Christ. But to
do that our thoughts must be focused on God's Word. We
must strive to see each situation and challenge from God's
perspective so that we might react to our momentary
challenges in a way that pleases Christ and builds up the
faith of others.

It is our choice to criticize or to find a reason to be
grateful. It is our choice to either claim our place as a
victim or speak God's Word as victors. We can either be an
individual that stirs up the fears and anxieties of those
around us, or we can be a calming influence. We can
choose to hold grudges and harbor the spirit of
unforgiveness, or we can trust in the providence of Jesus
Christ.

Remember, as mentioned previously, the thoughts
we hold on to will determine our decisions. Our decisions

will determine the actions we take. The actions we take will determine our outcomes. Our outcomes will determine our destiny. Are you walking in your God-ordained destiny? If not, go back to the beginning of the process and change the way you think and the thoughts you hold on to. What are you focused and fearless about?

Rules by Which to Engage Life

We can't take a magic pill to become a better leader and a person of positive impact. Reading this book can help, but remember that achieving your goals is not a one-time event. Being a good leader is a lifelong process. You will not have what you are unwilling to pursue. You must engage life. You must prepare. You must be persistent. You must be courageous and strong. You must embrace the pain of your transition if you are to achieve your significant goals and become the person Christ desires you to become. It is time for you to fulfill your spiritual destiny. The following "rules of engagement" for life can keep your thoughts focused on God's Word, and then the right decisions and actions will lead to the destiny God has prepared for you. You can be the best possible Christian leader and team member, to affect positively God's kingdom.

1. No Entitlements
You don't get a free pass because you are attractive, or because you have money, or because of the college you graduated from, or because of who your parents are. You have to earn everything through hard work and treating people appropriately.

2. Be Careful Who You Listen To

Not everyone deserves a front-row seat in your life. Some people, and maybe even some family members, who you love very much, have forfeited their right to speak into your life. They are not a positive influence on your life. Please escort those people from the front row to the balcony of your life. This does not mean that you have to stop loving them or necessarily talking to them. However, you do need to remove them as an influence in your life. Be careful who you allow to have your ear. Remember, what you think determines how you behave.

3. Become the Best "You" You Can Become

Do not spend a lot of time complaining about what is wrong. Spend more time doing what you can to make it better. Take responsibility for your part in the problem. Work on the areas in your life that need to improve to help provide the solution. Spend time working on you instead of telling others what is wrong with them.

There is a story about a king who went out into his palace garden. Unbelievably, he found that everything was withered and dying. The king examined the maple tree, which had withered up and was dying. He asked the maple tree what was wrong. The maple tree replied that it had given up because it wanted to be like the oak tree but was unable to. The king individually inspected all the plants in the garden, but they were all withering and dying. He asked each plant what was the problem, and they all replied they were quitting because they wanted to be something other than what they were but were unable to. The king was aghast. Where once a beautiful, lush garden thrived, incredibly now in its place was a shriveling, expiring clutter. Then out of the corner of his eye, the king saw a glimmer of bright color. He went to investigate and noticed a single violet. The violet was all alone, but vibrant and colorful. When asked why, in the midst of all that was withering and dying, it had chosen to thrive, the violet replied that it only wanted to be the best violet it could be. The violet told the king that when he was just a little seedling, its father said something it never forgot: "Be the best *you* that you can be. Others may do a greater work, but you have your part to do. And no one in all creation can do it as well as you."

4. Focus on the Long term
We always want what we want when we see it, and we see it now. We want what we want now, if at all possible. This speaks to our lack of control and our inability to say no, too often to the simplest things. When facing decisions, ask yourself these questions: "If this action comes to light, how will I feel about it?" "Will I think this is a smart move five years from now or ten years from now?" "Is this the action that honors Christ the most?" Do not bow to the gods of comfort, convenience, and predictability.

5. Focus on People, Not Possessions
Money doesn't make us happy; it just makes us more of what we already are. People are significantly more important than things, and when we focus on people, we have the opportunity to have both.

6. Focus on Problems, Not People
No one wakes up in the morning and says to him or herself, "Let me see just how much of a mess I can make of my day today." Everyone wants to succeed. They may not know how to go about doing it, but we all want to win. So face your day looking for the ways to solve problems and move forward, not letting conflict with people get in the way or getting caught trying to please everyone at the same time.

7. Discipline Yourself

Learn to control or correct yourself. Learn to "own the truth" about your choices, your thoughts, and your strengths and weaknesses. Learn to chasten or discipline yourself, for your benefit and those around you.

8. Focus on Substance, Not Looks

Everything that looks good is not good for you. Focus on those things that in their core contain goodness and provide positive long-term results.

9. Have a Humble Spirit

Don't think of yourself as better than anyone. Take time to know and appreciate those you perceive to be in a lower position than you, such as those who are less fortunate. Seek to always be willing to reach out and help those in need of a hand.

10. Do the Right Thing

No matter what the price, no matter what the perceived possible outcome, do the right thing. Make the biblical, godly choice.

11. Show Strength in Adversity

Life will deal us all some difficulty. It does rain on both the just and the unjust. Yet in adversity, we show His power. In adversity, we grow. In adversity, we prove the authenticity of our faith. Remember that adversity only appears to mock your commitment to Jesus Christ.

12. Live in Harmony with Those around You

In other words, live in alignment with the will and purpose of the organization and the function in which you work. Go out of your way to embrace those who are not like you, for this is the heart and spirit of God. Work hard to have the esteem of your loved ones. *Hold nothing back.*

13. *Be a Servant to Others*
Look to have a servant's heart, a heart that seeks to help and benefit others first. Look for ways to bless others, to accommodate others, to relieve others, and to make someone's life easier.

14. *Live a Life of Integrity*
Integrity is who you are when no one else is around. Who are you when you think no one is looking? Live a life that honors the positive, significant things of life.

15. *Don't Be Afraid to Stand Alone*
Don't be afraid to make the tough choices. Always choose to be obedient to God's Word, regardless of the consequences. Not everyone around you has a pure motive. When you stand for what is biblical and right, for what pleases Jesus and not men, people will leave you. But be encouraged, because some of the greatest things that will happen to you and for you will reveal themselves when you stand alone. Don't be afraid if people start to leave you and you find yourself without a lot of friends. It is the will of the Father, and He is preparing you for the next level of great abundance in your life. Look forward to spending time alone with the King.

16. *Do Excellent Work while No One Notices*
It is amazing how well we do our jobs when we think someone is going to inspect or notice what we are doing. We always want to make sure we get full credit for every small contribution we make. Do not be concerned if no one notices your efforts or if it seems you are not getting the results you want. Do not worry whether you get credit for

everything you do. Keep doing the will of the Father, for He sees your hard work and wants you to know your effort is not in vain. In due time, in due season, He will bless you with a blessing that will absolutely blow your mind, if you continue in excellence to His glory. Your effort will not prove to be unproductive.

17. Do What Others Will Not Do
Many people do not want an unglamorous job. They don't want a job that is not up front for all to see. Enthusiastically do whatever job you have been given with excellence, especially if it is a job others don't seem interested in. The Father has promised that He will show Himself strong and elevate your diligence and your passion for Him above those who think too highly of themselves.

18. Have a Correct Perspective about What Is Going on around You
Continue to "own the truth" about yourself, your loved ones, the situations you find yourself in, and the world around you. It is imperative that you have the correct reality as you are confronted with the choices of life. Remember God is always preparing, He is always testing, and He is always blessing.

Which three of these "rules of engagement" are you willing to improve to meet Christ's expectations for your service in ministry? How will you go about it?

_____

_____

_____

_____

_____

_____

_____

_____

_____

_____

_____

_____

_____

_____

_____

_____

_____

_____

_____

_____

Prayer of Forgiveness and Recommitment

Lord Jesus, I thank You for the revelations of this book for my life. I agree with You that I have not been the church member I should be. I choose to become the leader You desire. I recommit myself to Your Word, this ministry, and my pastor, and ask You to encourage me with Your Holy Spirit as I choose to love others as You have loved me. I thank You that I am a person of spiritual integrity. I thank You that I am the leader you have called me to be, in the name of Jesus. Amen!

Live the life you want to live. Be the person you want to remember.

Appendices

Disclaimer: The exercises and charts in the appendices that follow were collected from numerous sources and speakers over the past twenty years of study and ministry, therefore attempts to provide accurate documentation proved difficult. If any readers recognize material contained in the appendices and can identify original sources, please contact the author, Anthony Collins, through his website, www.WeBeenlLiedTo.com, so source documentation may be added at the next printing.

Appendix A
How Much Should Your Team Trust You?

Instructions: This questionnaire will help you assess how well your actions encourage the members of your team to place their trust in you. Answer these questions the way you think others on your team would answer if they were describing you. **Circle one number for each question.**

How often do you:	Almost Never	Seldom	Sometimes	Usually	Almost Always
	1	2	3	4	5

1. Meet agreed upon performance expectations?
2. Put the team's mission, goals and needs ahead of your own?
3. Share information?
4. Meet deadlines?
5. Honor agreed upon ground rules for working together?
6. Follow through on what you've said you will do?
7. Speak up when you disagree?
8. Make sure others receive the credit they deserve?
9. Volunteer for the hard jobs as well as the easy ones?
10. Address issues directly with the people concerned rather than avoid the issue or go to the team leader?
11. Take care not to exaggerate a problem?
12. Acknowledge when you don't know how to do something?
13. Admit when you've made a mistake?
14. Ask questions when you don't understand?
15. Admit when you're confused about your role or responsibilities?

How Much Should Your Team Trust You?

Based on your responses to the above questionnaire, decide what three actions you plan to take to increase the trust other team members have in you. List them below.

1. _____
   _____
   _____

2. _____
   _____
   _____

3. _____
   _____
   _____

Appendix B

Do You Have a Positive Christian Attitude?

Circle the score that corresponds with the correct answer for you for each question. Add each column, and then add the column totals. This is your final score.

	Almost Always	Sometimes	Almost Never
1. I can identify opportunities in new situations.	5	3	1
2. I am doubtful of new situations until proven.	1	3	5
3. I fear there's nothing better than my current situation.	1	3	5
4. I'm concerned that others won't be able to handle change.	1	3	5
5. I know I'll do well in a new situation.	5	3	1
6. I trust those responsible for implementing change.	5	3	1
7. I can't wait to see what's in store for each day.	5	3	1
8. I feel things are too good to be true and will certainly change today.	1	3	5

<u>Almost Always</u>   <u>Sometimes</u>   <u>Almost Never</u>

9. I'm not certain I'll get done what needs to get done today.
   1   3   5

10. I am confident the things I need to get done today will get done and done well.
   5   3   1

11. I feel like I'm going through the motions and wish something would happen to change things.
   1   3   5

12. I hope that my job is secure and my superiors think I'm doing okay.
   1   3   5

13. I look forward to finding new opportunities each new day.   5   3   1

14. I feel my church would say I have a good attitude.
   5   3   1

15. I don't allow the little things to bother me.
   5   3   1

16. I have had high enthusiasm toward my life and circumstances in the last few weeks.
   5   3   1

17. I believe my family would say I have a positive attitude.
   5   3   1

18. I would rate my attitude as positive.

              5   3   1

19. I've had no problem treating others with patience and sensitivity lately.

              5   3   1

20. I have had a high creativity level in the last few weeks.

              1   5   3

Column Totals

_____ + _____ + _____

Grand Total _____

Evaluate Your Score

90–100 = *Authentic Christian attitude.* You take a positive, proactive approach to most things you experience. You have a positive mental attitude. Focus on developing a system by which to maintain your current attitude or make it even better.

70–89 = *Can go either way.* You have good days and bad days in your attitude. Seek to develop a positive mental approach that will allow you to be positive proactively on a more consistent basis.

50–69 = *Your glass is definitely half empty.* You have a tendency to focus on the negative. You need a serious attitude tune-up. Develop some goals or a process to increase your positive attitude toward your circumstances each day. Seek biblical goals to learn a more positive approach.

0–40 = *Houston, we have a serious problem.* Negativity pervades your thoughts and feelings, and it is seriously holding you back in all aspects of your life. Seek help from God's Word and biblical counsel to find the root of your negativity, and then determine to change your attitude around, one step at a time.

* This questionnaire was adapted from *Attitude Is Everything*, Keith Harrell (London: Ebury & Vermilion, 2000).

Increase Your Positive Christian Attitude

Based on your responses in the questionnaire above, and the outcome of your final score, decide what actions you plan to take to increase your positive Christian attitude. List them below.

1. _____

   _____

   _____

2. _____

   _____

   _____

3. _____

   _____

   _____

Appendix C

Team Progress Checklist

For any project your team is responsible to complete, use the checklist below to evaluate progress during and after the project. Take this feedback and use it to improve your next performance and to stay on track with your team's ongoing mission and goals.

	Yes	No
1. Is everyone clear on the team's mission, goals, and performance standards?	☐	☐
2. Do you have the resources you need to complete the projects?	☐	☐
3. Do you have all the skills you need?	☐	☐
4. Do you have all the information you need?	☐	☐
5. Are you dealing with problems that may affect your ability to complete your mission and goals (for example, time or budget constraints, lack of suppliers, inability to meet performance standards, or interpersonal issues)?	☐	☐
6. Have you anticipated any changes that would affect your ability to complete your mission and achieve your goals?	☐	☐
7. Did you distribute the work fairly?	☐	☐
8. Do you have adequate access to management?	☐	☐
9. Are you making sound, informed decisions?	☐	☐
10. Are you looking for ways to improve what you're doing?	☐	☐

11. Are you documenting your team's process so you'll have the information for the future?

12. Are you checking with your customers as you go along?

13. Are you doing a good job of integrating new team members?

14. Have you adequately covered for anyone who has left the team or is absent?

15. Have you planned how to hand off this project when completed?

16. Are you effectively communicating your progress to the rest of the organization?

Appendix D

Exercise 1
Who Should Survive?

The following fifteen persons are in a bomb shelter. A worldwide nuclear event has taken place. The fifteen persons listed below are the only humans left alive on planet Earth. It will take two months for the radiation level outside to drop to a level where humans can withstand it and survive. The food and supplies in the shelter can sustain at a minimum level for only seven persons for two months. It is your task to decide the seven persons who will survive.

1. Dr. Wilson - 39, white, no religious affiliation, PhD in history, college professor, good health, married with one child (Bobby), active, enjoys politics.

2. Mrs. Wilson - 38, white, Jewish, AB and MA in psychology, counselor in a mental health clinic, good health, married with one child (Bobby), active in the community.

3. Johnny Wilson - 10, white, Jewish, in special education classes for four years mentally handicapped with IQ of 70, good health, enjoys his pets.

4. Mrs. Sanchez - 33, Spanish American, Roman Catholic, ninth grade education, cocktail waitress, prostitute, good health, married at 17, divorced at 18, abandoned as a child, in foster home as a youth, attacked by foster father at age 12, ran away from

home, returned to reformatory, stayed until 16, has one child who is three weeks old (Jean).

5. Rosa Sanchez - 3 weeks old, Spanish American, good health, nursing for food.

6. Mrs. Williams - 32, black, Protestant, AB and MA in elementary education, teacher, divorced, one child (Mary), good health, cited as outstanding teacher, enjoys working with children.

7. Mary Williams - 8, black, Protestant, third grade, good health, excellent student.

8. John Bearclaw- 13, Native American, eighth grade, good student, broad interests, good health, parents left reservation when teenagers.

9. Mr. Jackson - 25, black, claims to be an atheist, finishing last year of medical school, suspended, homosexual activity, good health, seems bitter about racial problems, wears hippy clothing.

10. Mrs. Bean - 28, black, Protestant, college graduate in engineering, electronics engineer, married, no children, good health, enjoys outdoor sports and stereo equipment, grew up in the ghetto.

11. Sis. Mary Catherine - 27, Catholic nun, college graduate, English major, grew up in middle-class neighborhood, good health, father is a businessman.

12. Mr. Washington - 51, white, Mormon, high school graduate, mechanic, "Mr. Fix- it," married, four children (not with him), good health, enjoys outdoors and working in his shop.

13. Miss Burgess - 21, Spanish American, Protestant, college senior, nursing major, good health, enjoys outdoor sports, likes people.

14 Father Tate - 37, white, Catholic priest, college plus seminary, active in civil rights, criticized for liberal views, good health, former college athlete.

15.Dr. Ricardo - 66, Spanish American, Catholic, medical doctor, general practitioner, has had two heart attacks in past three years but continues to practice.

Which seven people would you choose and why?

_____

_____

_____

_____

_____

_____

_____

Exercise 2

Have You Ever Judged a Book by Its Cover?

Read the following descriptions. Imagine that you are personally witnessing the situation and carefully think about and write down what your first impression might be of each person you encounter.

1. You are in line at the grocery store. In front of you is a woman who looks to be in her twenties, pregnant, with two small unkempt-looking children. You find yourself paying attention to the items she is purchasing and notice she is paying for her groceries with food stamps. She pays cash for the items the food stamps will not cover, which include two packs of cigarettes and some hair coloring.

2. You are driving through a commercial district during morning traffic in light rain. You notice the car in front of you has fishtailed at the last two traffic lights. You must stop so this car can parallel park, and because of traffic, you cannot pull around. After quite a few attempts, the driver parks successfully and emerges from the car. It is a woman with blonde hair.

3. You are driving down a busy street behind a black Ford pickup truck. On the rear window is a decal of Calvin urinating on the number 3. A bumper sticker reads: "My kid beat up your honor student." There is a gun rack affixed to the interior side of the rear window. As you get closer, you notice that on the very large arm resting outside the open driver's window is a tattoo of a snake.

4. As you ride in a car through an upscale neighborhood, you observe all the beautiful homes and landscaping. You then notice an adult black man running hurriedly on the boulevard.

5. Feeling the urge for a late-night snack, you and your friends pull into the 7-Eleven. Behind the counter is dark-skinned Middle Eastern–looking man with a nametag reading "Al-Habib."

6. You are following a car on the interstate. Traffic is sluggish, so you are following closely and at a slow enough speed to drive safely, while at the same time you observe the following bumper stickers on the car directly ahead of you: a Grateful Dead sticker; two bumper stickers, one that states, "If you're against abortion, have a vasectomy," and the other that states "Greenpeace."

7. It's time for you to buy some new cosmetics (if you are a male, imagine that it is time for your girlfriend, wife, or sister to buy cosmetics and you are accompanying her) and you decide to go to an upscale department store. You are greeted at the Chanel counter by a good-looking, well-groomed man with a nice smile, wearing a black smock over his clothing.

Do Your Thoughts and Feelings Honor God?

Based on your responses to the two diversity exercises above, what areas of concern do you have about your own preferences and prejudices? What areas do you need to improve upon? List them below.

Concerns:

_____

_____

_____

Improvements:

_____

_____

_____

Additional Thoughts:

_____

_____

_____

Appendix E

Case Study in Conflict:
Guess What's Happening in Bible Study

Samantha Jackson has been supervisor of the missions department of Praise Jesus Baptist Church for eleven years. Sam, as her friends call her, consistently receives high ratings from both her ministry leader and the congregation members who work with her on mission projects and trips. Recently, however, there have been rumors that Jackson has been having difficulty with Pedro Sanchez, the person in charge of the outreach ministry. The rumors have reached Bob Wilson, the executive pastor and Jackson's top supervisor.

Wilson decides to address the problem before things get really out of hand. He asks Jackson to see him on Sunday at 9 a.m. in his office. Jackson is puzzled by Wilson's rather curt request but decides not to read anything into it.

Sunday morning, promptly at 9 a.m., Jackson goes to Wilson's office. Wilson is talking to someone on the telephone and will not be available for about fifteen minutes, according to his secretary. Jackson sits down and cools her heels for more than thirty minutes. Finally Wilson buzzes his secretary and asks him to send Jackson in. When Jackson enters the office, before even saying good morning, Wilson asks, "What's this I hear about you and Sanchez having a fight?" Jackson is really taken aback, because while she and Sanchez had a difference of opinion about his going to the supplies supervisor without talking to her first, she certainly did not consider their encounter a fight. Wilson continues, "Sanchez says it is much more efficient for him to go directly to the supplies supervisor than to have to go through you, to me, to the pastor, and then the supplies supervisor. That makes sense to me too. So why are you making such a big deal about this?"

Conflict Case Study Response

What are the areas where the situation all went wrong?

_____

_____

_____

What similar pitfalls do you want to make sure to avoid in your current position?

_____

_____

_____

In this case study, what are the necessary steps to take to move forward positively?

_____

_____

_____

How can you take similar steps with your team to avoid potential areas of conflict?

_____

_____

_____

Live the life you want to live. Be the person you want to remember.

Author Note

If you would like to have the author to speak on or teach the principles contained in this book at your church or organization, or if this book has blessed you in any way, we would like to know. Leave us a note at www.WeBeenLiedTo.com.

Additional Resources from the Author

If you have enjoyed this book you may also enjoy two other books by this author. Both are available at Amazon.com or at the author's website www.WeBeenLiedTo.com.

The Ultimate Power Revealed in You
Foreword by Congressman John J. Duncan Jr.

100 Days of Inspiration
"For those who have experienced the storms of life"
http://www.bookstandpublishing.com/book_details/100_Days_of_Inspiration